TOILET TRAINING

without

TEARS or TRAUMA

Penny Warner, M.A.
Paula Kelly, M.D.

Meadowbrook Press
Distributed by Simon & Schuster
New York

Library of Congress Cataloging-in-Publication Data

Warner, Penny.
    Toilet training without tears or trauma / Penny Warner, Paula Kelly.
       p. cm.
    ISBN 0-88166-463-4 (Meadowbrook) ISBN 0-684-02019-X (Simon &
    Schuster)
       1. Toilet training. I. Kelly, Paula, M.D. II. Title.
    HQ770.5.W372003
    649.62—dc21

                                                        2003046413

Editorial Director: Christine Zuchora-Walske
Editor: Joseph Gredler
Proofreader: Angela Wiechmann
Production Manager: Paul Woods
Art Director: Peggy Bates
Cover Photo: © Peter Langone/ImageState
Illustrations: Susan Spellman
Index: Beverlee Day

Published by Meadowbrook Press, 5451 Smetana Drive, Minnetonka,
Minnesota 55343

www.meadowbrookpress.com

BOOK TRADE DISTRIBUTION by Simon & Schuster, a division of Simon
and Schuster, Inc., 1230 Avenue of the Americas, New York, New York 10020

07 06 05 04 03   8 7 6 5 4 3 2 1

Printed in the United States of America

Dedication

To Matt, Rebecca, Charley, Caitlin,
and Kelly, our diaper-free kids.

Acknowledgments

Many thanks to the parents who contributed their knowledge and tips to this book: Debbie Alegria, Gay Carter, Betty Clark, Kristy Dal Porto, Melanie Ellington, Kathleen Flanagan, Lanneau Grant, Becky Grewah, Kristin Grey, Manon Johnson, Suzanne Knoll, Holly Kralj, David Krumboltz, Rena Leith, Julie Long, Tamara Mader, Dana Mentick, Tracy Oliver, Esther Ong-Skerratt, Constance Pike, Gail Pike, Chris Saunders, Melissa Scheid, Meena Sheikh, Kelly Spruiell, Barbara Swec, Mia Thiele, Kay Van Houten, Mary Warner, Chloe Webster, Simonie Webster, and Susan Westerlund. And a special thanks to our editor, Joseph Gredler.

Contents

Introduction

It seems like only yesterday your toddler was a newborn infant, helpless and completely dependent on you. Your baby spent most of his early days nursing, sleeping, crying, and filling up diapers. Time flies, doesn't it? As a parent, you've experienced many exciting milestones since your baby's birth: the first time he looked at you, the first time he nursed, his first smile, first word, first step.

Now your baby is a toddler—walking, talking, laughing, playing, eating, drinking, and showing signs of greater autonomy each day. These are all important markers in your child's growth and development. One of the major milestones in your child's young life is moving from diapers to using the toilet. It's a big step for everyone involved.

As a child-development educator and pediatrician, our complementary professional backgrounds have helped us develop a simple, easy-to-use method to guide you through the toilet-training process. With an up-to-date understanding of child development and the latest information on what really works for parents, we're confident we can help you enjoy a stress-free, successful toilet-training experience. We believe that if you view toilet training as positive and challenging rather than negative and difficult, your end result will be rewarding instead of frustrating.

We understand that children between the ages of 22 and 36 months are more developmentally ready to take control of their bodily functions. After helping you confirm your child's readiness to toilet train, we emphasize a team approach in which your child takes control of the process and you assist by guiding, coaching, and cheering him on. We show you how creative techniques such as doll play can enhance the training process and actually make it fun. In addition, our innovative approach creates additional opportunities for your child to learn new and important skills beyond the basics of toilet training. Perhaps most importantly, we show you how to help your child feel good about learning to use the potty.

In Chapter 1, we discuss the history of toilet training and how attitudes have changed over the years. We also look at what recent studies tell us about parenting attitudes and what really works for parents. In Chapter 2, we explain the basic dos and don'ts of toilet training. We also help you assess your preconceptions about the process. In addition, we talk about child development, temperament types, and recommended language to use during toilet training. In Chapter 3, we focus on the signs of readiness your child should exhibit before toilet training begins. We also discuss the signs that indicate that your child is not ready.

In Chapter 4, we review the equipment you'll need, including potty-chairs, seat adapters, training pants, and other accessories. In Chapter 5, we provide tips and advice on preparing and planning for a positive experience. In Chapter 6, we help you begin the process by following our simple instructions. We encourage you to use lots of praise, role modeling, and doll play. In Chapter 7, we explain how repetition and practice can help keep the process fun and moving in the right direction. In Chapter 8, we help you troubleshoot problems that may develop, such as accidents, fears, power struggles, and bed-wetting. We also provide tips for helping your child stay dry all night.

Throughout the book you'll find helpful tips and reassuring anecdotes from parents who've successfully managed the toilet-training process with their children. In addition, you'll find Dr. Kelly's answers to the most commonly asked questions about toilet training. For your convenience, Appendix I provides checklists of the important topics covered in each chapter. Feel free to photocopy or tear out the lists and post them in a convenient spot in your home. Appendix II provides additional resources you may wish to consult, including books, videos, and Internet sites.

Chapter 1
Historical Perspectives

Toilet Training through the Decades

In the past, toilet training was often an anxious, even dreaded time for parents. The thought of eliminating diapers was frequently the only thing that kept parents motivated. In the 1920s, experts believed that infants could be conditioned to use the toilet. They encouraged parents to begin toilet training as early as the first few months, thinking a child's behavior could be conditioned by a parent's will and by behavior modification techniques. If parents failed to train their child by a certain age, they were considered a disappointment. This rigid and stressful approach, which failed to consider the child's point of view, often resulted in the training process taking much longer than necessary.

In the 1930s, early toilet training continued to be the norm as parents tried to control their child's elimination process instead of letting their child be the guide. Even the federal government promoted early training, issuing pamphlets that claimed, "Toilet training should begin by the third month and be completed by the eighth month."[1]

There were several reasons why parents went along with the experts' recommendations. First, parents had great respect for what doctors and other medical authorities said. Second, parents realized that early toilet training meant they wouldn't have to continue washing all those diapers, which at the time was done by hand. There were no diaper services or disposables back then, so keeping up with soiled diapers was often overwhelming. Parents (usually mothers) worked at the washer or scrub board a good part of the day making sure there were enough clean diapers for the baby.

In the 1940s, a more relaxed attitude began to emerge as doctors and psychologists began to fear that early toilet training could lead to physical and emotional problems for the child later in life. Parents were allowed to wait until their child was at least 9 months old before initiating training.

In the 1950s, attitudes changed even more as physicians advised parents to hold off on toilet training until their child's physical skills were more developed. This usually meant waiting until after the first year.

In the 1960s, psychologists, physicians, and other researchers studying child development began to realize that the *child* should be the one to decide when toilet training should begin—not the parents and not the experts. As a result, toilet-training philosophies began to shift away from the parents' desire to be rid of diapers toward a recognition of the child's level of readiness. Pediatricians began to encourage parents to wait for their child to show signs of readiness, which usually occurred between 18 and 24 months.

Social Pressures

In addition to expert opinions, social factors played a role in pressuring parents to begin toilet training before their child was ready. Many parents couldn't avoid comparing their child to other children. Parents sometimes felt disappointed if their child couldn't do things as early or as well as other children. Sometimes parents forgot that raising a child wasn't a competition with other parents, even though it may have felt that way at times. Some parents may have looked at their child's abilities as a reflection of their parenting skills. If their child wasn't keeping up with other children the same age, they may have considered themselves a failure. Many of these fears and concerns continue to trouble parents today.

Many parents today also feel pressured to begin training prematurely because of preschool admission requirements. Many preschools don't accept a child who isn't toilet trained, even though the child may be ready in every other respect. The staff may not want to deal with diapers, or the preschool may not be licensed to do so. If toilet training is rushed, a child may experience frequent accidents, which may cause embarrassment and regression.

Quick Tip

Be careful not to push your child too hard. I remember spending countless minutes in the bathroom saying, "Time to go potty!" while our son sat on the toilet. One time he kept saying, "No! I wanna do headstands!" After going back and forth for several minutes, I finally gave up and put him in the tub. A few minutes later, he climbed out and went potty by himself, even flushing the toilet. He can be a real rebel.

—Esther S.

Into the 21st Century: A Multitude of Methods

In the 1970s and 1980s, as more mothers began working outside the home, attitudes toward toilet training began to relax even more. Many books recommended waiting until shortly before the child's second birthday or later. However, each book offered a different method of training, and none took into account a child's unique circumstances and individual differences.

While many of the current books on toilet training promise success, their methodologies and premises are often flawed. Some of the philosophies are still rigid and stressful, and the information is sometimes inaccurate. Such methods often raise false hopes for parents and increase the stress of toilet training.

The Twenty-Four-Hour Method

This trendy approach makes a big promise: to have your child toilet trained in a single day. However, most parents who've tried this method know it's nearly impossible to train a child in a day. Attempting to do so often leads to frustration and disappointment, both for the child and the parents. Young children have short attention spans; they need lots of time and repetition to practice developing skills. A speeded-up method creates unnecessary stress and often ends in failure.

The Multiple-Choice Method

Another popular book on the market offers parents several approaches to toilet training: "The Readiness Approach," "The Early Approach," "The Fast Approach," and "The Intense Approach." With so many choices, parents may be confused about which one is best for their child. They may find the information contradictory and the advice overwhelming.

The Picture Book Method

Several picture books are also available to help kids learn to use the toilet. While picture books are great at getting children excited about using the toilet, they offer little in the way of advice and information to help parents train their kids. This is true for many videos on the market as well.

Quick Tip

When I decided it was time for my son to be toilet trained, I tried one method after another. Nothing worked. I was getting really frustrated. Then a friend told me about the stress-free training method. The first thing I learned was that my child wasn't ready.

So I put the whole thing on the back burner and waited for him to show real signs of wanting to use the toilet. When he finally did, everything else fell into place. What a difference.

—Connie P.

The Latest Studies

Dr. T. Berry Brazelton believes that early training is nothing more than anticipating a baby's reflexive release of urine or feces at the right moment. Parents may *think* their child is controlling her bladder or bowels, but this is probably not the case. Dr. Brazelton feels that toilet training is best delayed until the end of the second year or beginning of the third year, when a toddler can consistently identify signals from a full bladder or rectum and can wait until she gets to the toilet before allowing the muscles to relax.

Two-year-olds are also more likely to be cognitively, psychologically, socially, and emotionally prepared for toilet training. Research indicates that parents who postpone toilet training until after the second birthday are usually successful within four months.[2] Statistics also show that 90 percent of children between the ages of 24 and 30 months succeed in toilet training, with the average age being 27–28 months.[3] Eighty percent of children gain nighttime success between the ages of 30 and 42 months, with 33 months being the average age.

As previously mentioned, starting too early often lengthens the process and makes it more stressful. Statistics show that 50 percent of children who begin toilet training at 18 months or earlier don't achieve reliable control until 36 months or later.[4] Early training can also cause long-term problems such as constipation, bed-wetting, and guilt. In addition, forcing a child who isn't ready may result in unnecessary power struggles. A child may become frustrated, angry, and resentful, causing major setbacks in the process.

In a comprehensive toilet-training study presented at the Pediatric Academic Societies' Annual Meeting in 1999, experts identified three important phases in the toilet-training process:[5]

1. Recognizing when a child is ready to start toilet training
2. Switching from diapers to disposable or cloth training pants
3. Training the child using proven techniques

In the study, researchers questioned parents of 267 children ages 15–42 months on a number of toilet-training issues. Results showed that most parents began toilet training when their child showed signs of readiness, such as staying dry during a nap, being interested in the toilet, and following simple directions. Parents often used positive reinforcement, praise, and reminders during the toilet-training process. They also made the potty-chair easily accessible. In addition, most parents used a firm but friendly tone to encourage their child to be a "big kid."

Although the study reported considerable variation in the length of time to train, the majority of children (64 percent) were in the slow or intermediate group, meaning training took longer than the average time. The average duration of toilet training was eight to ten months, including starts and stops.

There were minor differences between boys and girls. On average, girls trained earlier than boys: Girls were just under three years old while boys were three years and three months. According to the study, factors such as daycare, parents working outside the home, number of siblings, or marital status did not affect the speed of toilet training.

According to another study, 4 percent of children were trained by age two, 60 percent by age three, and only 2 percent were not trained by age four.[6] This further indicates that the majority of children learn to use the toilet between two and three years of age.

Quick Tip

When my son turned three and was still in diapers, I was really worried that he might never use the toilet. All his friends were wearing big-boy pants and going to the toilet regularly, but my son just didn't seem to care. Finally, I read an article that said many kids were still in diapers at age three—and this was normal! It made me feel so much better. I think when I began to relax, he began to show more interest in the toilet.

—Melanie E.

How Do Today's Parents View Toilet Training?

A peek at a recent study of parents' attitudes toward toilet training reveals changes that have occurred over the decades.[7] It also tells us a lot about what parents think and feel about the process.

How do today's parents compare to their parents when it comes to toilet training?

The majority of parents (60 percent) used the same or similar techniques their parents used on them, while 40 percent differed substantially in their views about toilet training.

When do most parents begin to train their children?

Approximately half of the parents began toilet training when their child showed signs of readiness. About one-fourth started when their child was a certain age. Less than 5 percent used factors such as preschool deadlines, new babies coming, or peer pressure to initiate toilet training.

What's the most common age to begin toilet training?

Thirty-one percent of parents began training when their child was 18–22 months old. Twenty-seven percent began when their child was 23–27 months old. Sixteen percent began when their child was 28–32 months old. Twenty-two percent began when their child was 32 months or older.

What's the most common sign of readiness?

Twenty-eight percent of parents said their child's interest in the toilet got the process started. Twenty-five percent reported their child's aversion to being wet or soiled got things going. Nineteen percent said the process began with their child's use of words, body language, or facial expressions. Eighteen percent reported that their child's desire to wear big-kid pants was the motivating factor.

Who initiates toilet training?

Over half the parents reported that they initiated the process together with their child. Only 14 percent of parents initiated alone, while 28 percent reported that their child was the one to initiate.

What's the most common sign of commitment to toilet training?

For most parents (46 percent), buying and trying out the new potty-chair was the first official sign that their child was committed to toilet training. Twenty-eight percent said it was when their child first put on transition clothing or diapers. About 10 percent said that reading a toilet-training picture book to their child signaled a commitment to toilet training.

What type of toilet do kids prefer?

Thirty-six percent of children preferred the child-size potty. Twenty-six percent preferred the standard toilet, 24 percent preferred the adapter seat, and the rest preferred some combination. Most kids liked their potty-chairs decorated with stickers.

What are the most common words used in toilet training?

For urination, almost half the kids used *pee-pee*, 22 percent used *go potty*, 18 percent used *pee*, and 4 percent liked *tinkle*. For defecation, about a third used *poo-poo* while another third used *poop. Ca-ca* was favored by less than 10 percent, while the rest used their own special words.

What rewards are best?

Half of the parents used praise when helping their child learn to use the toilet. Fifteen percent used candy, 9 percent used special privileges, 7 percent used toys, 2 percent used money, and the rest used other rewards.

What are children's most common fears about toilet training?

Fear of the toilet is very real for kids. Thirty-five percent were afraid of falling into the toilet, 14 percent didn't like the idea of things leaving their bodies, and 6 percent feared flushing. The rest had a variety of fears.

What are the differences between boys and girls?

Seventy-five percent of parents felt girls were easier to train, while the remaining 25 percent felt that boys were easier. As for style, the debate over sitting and standing was divided. A little over 50 percent of the boys preferred sitting, while a little under half liked to stand. Almost half the girls had tried standing at least once!

How often do children regress after beginning toilet training?

A quarter of the children who began toilet training didn't return to diapers. Forty-five percent went back to diapers for a short time, 17 percent started the process over at least once, 17 percent started over twice, and 35 percent started over so many times their parents stopped counting! The majority of parents (84 percent) experienced setbacks in toilet training, primarily because the child lost interest (about 57 percent). Over half the children had deliberate accidents during the process.

What are the biggest problems with toilet training?

Thirty-one percent of parents reported that traveling was the biggest disruption to toilet training. Twenty-six percent said that nighttime was the biggest problem. Twenty-one percent reported that shopping was the major problem. The remaining parents cited issues such as daycare problems and friends visiting during daytime hours.

How do parents feel when their child is finally toilet trained?

Forty percent of parents were proud that their child took another major step toward independence. Thirty-four percent were relieved the process was finally over. Twenty-six percent had mixed feelings about the fact that their child was no longer a baby.

Quick Tip

To me, toilet training was not about training my child but about training myself. Jordan was three and still in diapers, with the first day of preschool looming ahead. I tried several times to get him trained, but he continued to have accidents. I was at the point of panic. When the first day of preschool arrived, I got brave and sent him to school in big-boy underpants. From that day on there were no accidents! But the fear of that first day will live with me forever.

—Lanneau G.

Chapter 2
Getting Started

Good Reasons to Begin Toilet Training

Aside from the obvious (no diapers, less mess), you'll want to examine your motives for wanting to toilet train your child at this particular time. Here are some good reasons to begin, once your child is ready.

Independence

You want to foster autonomy in your child so he'll eventually become an independent person.

Self-Esteem

You want your child to feel good about himself by increasing his competence and confidence.

Teamwork

You want to approach toilet training as a team and work together to help your child reach this significant milestone.

Not-So-Good Reasons to Begin Toilet Training

Many parents are faced with very real pressures to begin toilet training. However, it's best to avoid allowing these pressures to dictate the timing.

Peer Pressure

Don't let family and friends pressure you to train your child. That decision should be made by you and your child, not someone else.

Preschool Admittance

If your child isn't ready to move out of diapers, you're asking for trouble. Preschool can wait. On the other hand, if you think your child is ready and you'd like to start him in preschool, a little encouragement may be all he needs.

Another Baby Coming

Don't try to force toilet training because you're expecting a new baby. If your child isn't ready, it won't happen. It would be nice to have only one child in diapers at a time, but you'll get there eventually. Besides, children who aren't fully trained by the time a new baby arrives often regress to diapers. Be patient.

Being a Super Parent

Your child's ability to use the toilet is not a reflection of your parenting skills. It's a matter of your child's readiness, not your parenting skill.

Diaper Expense

Every parent would love to eliminate diapers from the shopping list. However, if your child isn't ready, you may end up prolonging the process, which will only add to the expense.

Techniques That Don't Work

Some techniques are not only ineffective, they're potentially harmful to a child's psyche and self-esteem.

Forcing

Trying to make your child use the toilet when he's not ready only leads to power struggles, tears, and anger. It may even cause physical problems such as constipation.

Shaming

Children who are shamed into using the toilet may have toileting problems later in life, not to mention guilt, antisocial behavior, and lowered self-esteem. Don't call your child names, use negative terms, tease, or tell him he's bad if he doesn't use the toilet.

Spanking

Corporal punishment may appear to change a child's behavior in the short term, but the effects are usually temporary. Also, spanking may cause low self-esteem and regression. It's best to use positive reinforcement, like praise and rewards.

Sitting for Long Periods of Time

Making your child sit on the toilet for long periods of time may cause him to dislike the toilet and want to avoid using it. Your child may become bored, restless, cranky, and uncooperative, and he may begin to undermine your efforts by wetting himself before you have a chance to put him on the toilet.

Running Water

Running water is a psychological technique that may work for older people as a trained response, but the sound doesn't do much for younger children. You just end up wasting water.

Don't push your child into using the toilet too early. Our three-year-old let us know when she was ready, and we had very few accidents or setbacks. We bought a child-size potty, explained what it was, and waited until she wanted to use it. A child has a strong desire to be like Mommy and Daddy.

—Kristin G.

A Parent's Perspective: Exploring Your Preconceptions

The way you were toilet trained may influence your attitude about the process. Any toileting problems you may have had (or still have) may shape your expectations. For example, you may expect your child to train in a matter of hours, since your mother claimed you were trained in a very short time. You may believe that once your child has used the toilet successfully, he won't return to diapers. You may think that toilet training is a matter of attitude (rather than physical, cognitive, and psychological readiness) and wonder why your child is not cooperating.

Trauma

If you had a bad experience during toilet training, such as being shamed, punished, or ridiculed, you may harbor some anxiety about the process. You may want to talk to your doctor or another trained professional about ways to manage this anxiety.

Embarrassment

If you feel uncomfortable or embarrassed about the thought of bodily functions, or if you don't like talking about them, you may struggle when dealing with your child's toilet training. Try to decide which words you'd be comfortable using during the training process. (See page 20.)

Anxiety

If you're worried or frightened about how to begin or what to do, you need to identify and address your concerns. If you try to hurry the process and become tense and anxious while training your child, or if you lose your cool and become impatient, you may end up prolonging the process.

Accidents

If you can't accept the fact that accidents will happen as your child is learning to control his muscles, you'll create unnecessary stress and possibly impede the process. Try to relax and take accidents in stride. (See page 70.)

Patience

If you don't agree that toilet training takes time, repetition, positive reinforcement, and patience, you're likely to experience frustration and failure.

Punishment

If you think your child needs to be punished in order to learn a new skill, you're bound to have problems. If you see the process as a teaching opportunity, you're likely to find it exciting, rewarding, and fun. This doesn't mean you should be overly relaxed and permissive in your training. Your child needs guidance. But that's where you—and your teaching skills—come in.

Quick Tip

When I was a child, I remember sitting on the toilet for what seemed like hours trying to pee, and it would never come—not until I was OFF the toilet, of course. That just made my mother madder. I didn't get out of diapers until I was four, mainly because I grew to hate the toilet, just sitting there with all that pressure. I promised myself I'd keep the process positive for my kids, even if it took longer.

—Chloe W.

Understanding Child Development

An important part of the toilet-training process is understanding your child's point of view, developmental level, and learning style. Children develop at different rates and in different ways. Some children learn quickly; others take more time. Your child needs to learn at his own pace; he can't be rushed. Learning to use the toilet is a rite of passage that helps a child feel independent. It gives him power and control over his body, and it helps him take another step toward becoming an autonomous individual.

Parents also need to realize that children are often fascinated by their bodily functions, especially elimination and defecation. Parents have learned to take these things for granted, so they need to make an effort to see the world from their child's point of view. For example, a child may see his feces as a part of his body, and he may be frightened when that part is flushed away. Most children are interested in their body parts and curious about what they do. Parents can take advantage of this natural curiosity when training their child to use the toilet.

Most children find the toilet fascinating in a generally positive way. Some kids, however, are afraid of the toilet and wonder where all that stuff goes when it swirls around and disappears. Your child may see the toilet as a scary monster, a strange object, a curious receptacle, an exciting plaything, or even a boring nonentity. Some kids try to flush things down the toilet in an effort to understand how it works. Other kids may be attracted to every new toilet they see, and they may even do a "territorial marking" that gives them a sense of control. Parents need to work with their child to communicate clearly in simple terms what toilets are used for.

Temperament Types

Your child's temperament also plays an important role in how he learns to use the toilet. Forty percent of children are considered "easy." They're flexible, not easily disturbed by noise and other interruptions, and they have generally pleasant dispositions. Fifteen percent are considered "slow to warm up." They have trouble adapting to new situations, take time to adjust, and move at their own pace. Ten percent are considered "challenging." They have irregular habits, show intense emotions, and are easily disturbed by noises and other interruptions. The rest have a mixture of these basic temperaments. Here's a breakdown of children's basic temperament features and how they might affect the timing and success of toilet training.[8]

Activity Level

Some children are active all the time, while others are less so. Active children usually have a harder time focusing on toilet training because they're always busy; less active children usually adapt more quickly. If your child is active, help bring his attention to the task by focusing on the toilet and eliminating outside distractions.

Rhythmicity

Some children have regular cycles of activity (eating, sleeping, and defecating on schedule), while others are less predictable. If your child has regular habits, he'll probably be easier to train. Less predictable children make the job trickier, so you may have to tune in to your child's schedule rather than have him follow yours.

Approach and Withdrawal

Some children delight in new experiences, while others withdraw from them. If your child enjoys new things, he'll probably adjust readily to using the toilet. If he tends to withdraw from new situations, he'll need more encouragement.

Adaptability

Some children adjust readily to changes in their routine, while others are unhappy with disruptions. If your child adapts well, he'll likely be easier to train. If not, he'll need more guidance, encouragement, and flexibility.

Intensity of Reaction

Some children express their feelings openly when experiencing an emotion, while others tend to be more reserved. If your child communicates his feelings readily, he may need some soothing and guidance in learning to manage his emotions. If your child is cautious, he may need some help expressing himself.

Threshold of Responsiveness

Some children's senses are more sensitive than others. A sensitive child may startle at the sound of a flushing toilet. Other children are less affected by unexpected noises and other sensory disruptions. If your child seems particularly sensitive, be wary of flushing the toilet. If he doesn't seem particularly sensitive, let him flush the toilet. See how he reacts.

Quality of Mood

Some children seem constantly happy and ready to embrace life, while others seem guarded and ready to protest at any moment. If your child is generally happy, he'll probably enjoy learning to use the toilet. If he's reticent, he may be more reluctant.

Distractibility and Attention Span

Some children are easily distracted, while others are able to focus their attention for longer periods of time. If your child is easily distracted, he may not be ready to focus on learning to use the toilet. To help him, minimize distractions, use a potty-chair that holds his attention (such as a musical chair or one decorated with stickers), and read toilet-training books while he sits on the potty. If he has a good attention span, he'll be better able to concentrate on the task.

My child was afraid of big toilets. He could handle the potty-chair because it was his size, but big toilets seemed to overwhelm him. He would draw pictures of them, but he wouldn't go near them. I think his drawings helped him overcome his fears, because eventually he quit drawing big toilets after he learned to use them.
—Kay V.

The Disabled Child

If your child has a physical, mental, or emotional disability, the challenge of toilet training may be even greater. In addition to your child's individual needs, developmental level, and ability to learn new tasks, you'll have to take into account his specific disability. The good news is that most disabled children are able to toilet train. However, the process may have to be delayed, and it may take longer to complete.

You should talk to your child's physician, specialist, therapist, or other trained professional about your child's situation. They may know a particular technique that's been helpful with other children with the same or a similar disability.

Be prepared to slow down the pace of training, and expect setbacks along the way. Disabled children may need additional help developing the skills needed for toilet training, including fine and gross motor abilities, attention span, and motivation.

It may help to break down the training process into simple steps. Have your child practice each step several times before progressing to the next level. For example, you may want to have your child practice pulling down his pants before having him try to pull them up again. Don't forget to provide lots of praise and rewards along the way.

You can find custom-made potty-chairs at medical supply stores, through your physical therapist, and through websites such as www.ataccess.org and www.ablegeneration.com. Specially designed potty-chairs provide grab bars, safety rails, chest straps, seat belts, armrests, height adjustments, wheelchair conversions, adaptive toilet seats, and other forms of assistance.

Toilet Talk

The language you use in toilet training is important in helping your child understand what's happening and what things are called. Most experts recommend using simple terms rather than adult vocabulary. For urination, common choices include *pee, pee-pee, wee-wee,* and *tinkle.* For defecation, popular words include *poo, poo-poo, poopie, doo-doo, BM,* and *ca-ca.* Feel free to use other words that have been used by your family or friends.

Some parents prefer terms that are less direct, such as *use the bathroom, go to the toilet,* or *make potty.* This is sometimes done to avoid embarrassment or the discomfort associated with words that refer to bodily functions. However, such indirect terminology may confuse your child, since it's less precise. It's best to use language that clearly communicates what you're referring to.

Quick Tip

I was a little embarrassed about toileting terminology, and I'm sure my child could sense this. I kept referring to "number one" and "number two," but that didn't seem to make any sense to him. One day I heard my friend ask her child if he needed to go pee-pee or poo-poo. My son started repeating the words over and over, probably because they were fun to say. Anyway, I joined in and pretty soon we were using those terms when he had to go to the toilet. I still get embarrassed when he says them in the middle of the grocery store at the top of his lungs, but I'm glad he knows what they mean!

—Barbara S.

Ask Dr. Kelly

Question: My mother-in-law insists that all her children were trained by 12 months. She seems to be implying that we are miserable failures as parents, since our two-and-a-half-year-old son is not yet trained. Have we done something wrong? If not, how do we deal with this kind of pressure?

Answer: It may or may not be true that your mother-in-law's children were trained by their first birthday. Time and memory sometimes distort the facts. Regardless, you can explain to her, as diplomatically as possible, that toilet-training philosophies have changed over the years. Current recommendations emphasize waiting until a child shows signs of readiness. You can even show her the information in this book if you feel it might help.

Question: My wife often uses words like *yucky, stinky,* and *icky* when smelling or changing our daughter's diaper. I thought I heard somewhere that this isn't advisable. Is this true?

Answer: You're right, although your wife's behavior is quite common. Urine and feces are best viewed as normal byproducts of eating and digestion. They should not be described with words or a tone of voice that creates negative impressions in a child's mind. Such words can contribute to a child's fear of using the toilet, and may cause a child to distance himself from the toilet-training process. I support you in trying to avoid these words. Ask your wife if language such as, "It's diaper time!" or, "Let's make a change!" doesn't make more sense.

Question: Our first child was a terror to train. Despite my strong intention to avoid a power struggle, it turned into a royal battle. He was three-and-a-half before we finally got there. Our second son, however, woke up one morning, announced his desire to use the toilet, and was out of diapers from that day on. What a breeze! How can two kids be so different?

Answer: I often hear that different children from the same family train differently. On average, first-born children tend to train at older ages than their siblings. Also, boys tend to train later than girls. I think many parents try to exert too much control with their first child. The process is often delayed until the power struggle is abandoned. Second-born children also have the benefit of the older child as a role model, and they're often excited to join the ranks of the potty trained.

Question: When I take my son in for his well-child exams, I usually come prepared with questions to make the best use of the time with the doctor. When should I raise the issue of toilet training?

Answer: As you're probably aware, the frequency of well-child visits decreases as a baby becomes a toddler—just when parents are likely to need advice on issues such as toilet training! This is because the scheduling of visits is based largely on the immunization schedule, not on a parent's need for guidance. As a pediatrician, I try to begin a conversation with parents when their child is 15–18 months old, and for sure by 21–24 months. At the one-year checkup, I try to mention that we'll be discussing toilet training in upcoming visits. Even though the child may not be ready to train for several months, I think it's appropriate to initiate a discussion, especially about signs of readiness. I also talk to parents at the three- and four-year checkups, either to provide helpful suggestions or to make sure training is going well.

Chapter 3
Signs of Readiness

Over the years, experts have changed their opinions about the perfect time to train a child. So how do you know when to begin? When your mother reminds you she toilet trained her children at one year? When your child is headed off to a preschool that requires her to be toilet trained? When you realize you've already changed five thousand diapers?

Although most experts would agree that trying to train a toddler before the age of two is not recommended, there is no perfect age for all children. The majority of children display a window of readiness between 18 months and three years, depending on their maturity level. Given this wide range, you have to look for specific signs that your child is ready to train.

Readiness depends not only on your child's individual maturation rate but also on her temperament and interest. If your child is not ready, trying to force the issue will only lead to battles and rebellion. If you let your child take the lead, the experience will likely be positive instead of stressful.

Quick Tip

We had a child in our preschool who was three-and-a-half and showing all the signs of having to use the potty. One day I asked him if he was doing the "pee-pee dance," and he said, "No, I'm just relaxing." After a few more minutes of doing the dance, he began to realize that he had to go to the potty. He just needed a little reminder to trigger his awareness.

—Manon J.

Let Your Child Be the Guide

How do you help your child take the lead when it comes to toilet training?

First Comes Awareness

You can begin by looking for three general levels of awareness:

1. *Has wet.* Your child is aware that she has wet or filled her diaper.

2. *Is Wetting.* Your child is aware that she's in the process of wetting or filling her diaper.

3. *Will Wet.* Your child is aware that she's about to wet or fill her diaper.

As a general rule, the higher the level of awareness, the more likely the child is ready to begin training. Once you've identified your child's general level of awareness, the next step is to look for more detailed signs of readiness in the areas of physical, cognitive, and psycho-social-emotional development.

Developmental Stages

There are three main areas of child development: physical, cognitive, and psycho-social-emotional. Your child must be ready in all three areas in order to have a successful toilet-training experience. If you study your child for signs that she's mastered the essential physical skills and demonstrated the necessary level of awareness, toilet training should go smoothly. Be ready to offer your child guidance, motivation, and positive reinforcement to help her accomplish this major milestone, and let her know that you're confident she'll do it. You may have days when you think she'll *never* be ready, but rest assured that she'll get there when the time is right.

Whenever I got discouraged while toilet training my child, I remembered what my mother told me about my own toilet training: "I thought you'd NEVER get out of diapers. You never seemed ready or interested. And look at you now—diaper free!" Just keep things in perspective and relax.

—Betty C.

Physical Signs of Readiness

One of the first ways you can tell that your child might be ready for toilet training is observing her physical ability and behavior. Here's a list of the basic physical skills that will be needed for a successful experience.

Gross Motor Skills

Your child can use her arms and legs to climb on and off the big toilet using a stepstool, or she can sit comfortably on a potty-chair.

Elimination Patterns

Your child's bowel movements have become more regular and predictable, and she stays dry during the day for longer periods of time.

Manual Dexterity

Your child can pull her pants up and down with little or no help.

My daughter had excellent fine motor control for her age. She could do fairly difficult tasks with her hands and fingers, such as coloring and doing puzzles. But her gross motor control was weak. She preferred to sit and play rather than climb and run and jump. I realized she needed encouragement to develop her large-muscle skills, so we began by having her dress her dolly, which she was good at. Then I encouraged her to try pulling down her own pants, and pulling them up again. After several tries, she started to get the hang of it. That really helped when it came time to use the potty.

—Gail P.

Cognitive Signs of Readiness

More subtle signs of readiness are apparent in the way your child thinks and communicates.

Sensory Awareness

Your child seems to know when she's urinating or defecating, or is sensitive to being wet or soiled.

Good Attention Span

Your child can focus on a task for several minutes at a time.

Ability to Follow Simple Directions

Your child can understand and follow simple directions such as, "Please pull down your pants and sit on the potty."

Communication Skills

Your child can tell you in her own way that she's urinated or defecated or that she has to use the toilet. She can use words such as *I go pee-pee* or can communicate nonverbally by pulling at her pants or doing something similar.

Understanding of Terminology
Your child understands the language used for toilet training and for describing her body parts.

Understanding the Concept of Using the Toilet
Your child knows what the toilet is used for.

Dislike of Being Wet
Your child doesn't like the feeling of being wet or soiled and wants to be changed.

Quick Tip

My son had a language delay, thanks to a lot of ear infections. He wasn't very talkative, but he was great at gestures. He let me know he needed to use the potty by pointing toward it and pulling at his pants. Eventually he started to use the words, but gesturing helped prevent him from getting frustrated until his language caught up. I encourage parents to teach their babies simple gestures to help enhance communication and facilitate language development.
—Chris S.

Psycho-Social-Emotional Signs of Readiness
Finally, watch for signs that your child has a sense of herself, is socially aware, and is emotionally ready to go through the toilet-training process.

Self-Awareness
Your child demonstrates her sense of self by saying "me" or "mine," by displaying her toys, and by showing pride in her accomplishments.

Curiosity about the Toilet

Your child wants to know more about toilet training and is interested in watching others use the toilet.

Ability to Imitate Someone Using the Toilet

Your child imitates the actions of parents or siblings by sitting on the small toilet and pretending to use it.

Emotional Stability

Your child is mostly beyond the "negative" stage of development. In addition, she's not experiencing any traumatic events such as adjusting to a new baby, a new home, or her parents' divorce.

Receptivity to Praise

Your child is eager to please others, she beams when praised, and she enjoys succeeding at new tasks.

Eagerness to Be a "Big" Kid

Your child is interested in wearing training pants or underpants instead of diapers, and she knows she's not a baby anymore.

Ability to Engage in Imaginative Play

Your child likes to pretend to have her stuffed animal or doll use the toilet, and she understands the basic procedures.

Quick Tip

My son wanted to wear big-boy pants so badly, he practically trained himself how to use the toilet. Of course, it probably helped to have two older brothers as role models. I'm sure he wanted to be just like them! If you don't have older siblings, cousins, or neighborhood kids available to play with your child and show him how to use the potty, try to find other ways such as play groups, play dates, daycare, and preschool.

—Mary W.

Signs That Your Child Is *Not* Ready

Although your child may exhibit some of the signs of readiness, she may show other signs that tell you she's not quite there yet.

Lack of Awareness

Your child seems oblivious to the fact that she's wet or soiled, or she doesn't seem to sense when she's urinating or defecating.

Lack of Interest

Your child doesn't seem to show any interest in her diaper, the potty-chair, the big toilet, or anything related to using the toilet.

Frequent Urination

Your child wets her diaper every hour or two during the day. (Chances are she's not ready to hold her urine long enough to succeed at toilet training.)

Resistance

Your child resists your attempts to encourage her to use the toilet, either by saying so, by getting angry, by crying, or by running away.

Negativity

Your child is still in the "negative" stage of development (what some people call the "terrible twos"). Experts actually consider this a positive stage in which a child asserts her independence.

Stress

Your child is experiencing a stressful event such as a new baby arriving, a move to a new home, a change in daycare, a death in the family, and so on.

Disability

Your child has a disability, such as a developmental delay or a physical handicap, which is impeding the process. (See pages 19–20.)

My sister-in-law had a baby boy a year or so before I did. She told me she had him potty trained by the end of his first year. So, of course, I had to compete with her. But I was a total failure. Exhausted and hysterical, I went to my doctor to find out what was wrong. He had a good laugh and told me my sister-in-law's baby wasn't really toilet trained at one year. He had regular elimination habits, and his mother was able to put him on the toilet at the right time, which gave her the impression that he was trained.

—Rena L.

Doll Play

Another way to assess your child's readiness is to enlist the help of one of your child's dolls or stuffed animals, preferably one that can be diapered and clothed. Some dolls are designed to "drink" and "wet," and some are anatomically correct. Using a doll in imitative play can give your child a chance to display her skills and thoughts about toilet training without putting all the attention and pressure on herself.

Through doll play, you can observe your child showing an interest in using the toilet, or you can encourage her to imitate you or an older sibling using the toilet and being "grown-up." Your child's eagerness to engage in doll play can be seen as a strong indicator of readiness.

Sample Dialogue for Doll Play

While playing house or having a tea party with your child and her doll or teddy, try initiating an exchange with the following words: "It's been a while since we checked Dolly's diaper. Should we look to see if it's time to change Dolly into a clean diaper?" This creates the opportunity for your child to show an interest in the topic. If your child wants to change her doll's diaper, then show her how to do it, help her do it, or let her do it herself. Make sure to explain what's happening and why it needs to be done.

After you've introduced the concept of needing to be changed, you might take the doll play to the next level with the following words: "Oh my! I think Dolly's diaper is wet! I bet she wants to feel dry and comfy again. We better change her. Do you think Dolly might want to use the potty-chair to go pee-pee or poopie, now that she's getting to be such a big girl?" Your child's response and attitude will indicate her level of interest in the subject.

Quick Tip

Before we started toilet training our two-and-a-half-year-old daughter, we used to sit on the toilet seat together and make a swishing noise to re-create the sound of urinating. When we had her sit on the toilet alone and make the sound, she was able to pee.

—Meena S.

Ask Dr. Kelly

Question: My child's preschool guidelines state that children must be toilet trained before they can attend. The fall start date is fast approaching, and my three-year-old son is still having an occasional accident in his underwear, especially if he's preoccupied with a toy or activity. He loves his big-boy pants and is very proud of his ability to use the toilet, but I'm afraid he'll get so absorbed in preschool activities that he'll have an accident and be dismissed! What should I do?

Answer: You may want to have a private conversation with the school administrators about how strict the policy is. Many administrators are flexible and open-minded about this transitional period. In fact, they expect a recently trained child to experience setbacks when starting school. Many preschools encourage parents to send a change of clothes or two in case of accidents. They also provide ample potty breaks, frequent reminders, and easy access to the bathrooms. If a preschool's policy seems too rigid, you may want to look at other schools. A too-rigid philosophy may carry over into other areas as well. Keep in mind that children naturally want to be like their peers. Your child may surprise you at his success while at school.

Question: My father tells me I have trouble setting limits with my son, and he thinks this will prevent me from being able to toilet train him effectively. He even asked if he could take over the responsibility! What should I do?

Answer: Having problems setting limits can make toilet training more difficult. However, you can view the process as an opportunity to review and improve your relationship with your child. Parents *and* grandparents need to know that the *child* has the real authority in determining when toilet training will occur. If guiding the process has resorted to pressures and the need for constant reminders, it's probably best to stop for a few months. After that, you can reassess your child's readiness and decide what to do. Don't hesitate to seek help with discipline if you're struggling in that department. What you learn will likely improve the toilet-training process.

Question: Our two-and-a-half-year-old daughter seems to be showing some of the signs of readiness I've read about, such as asking to have her diaper changed after she's had a BM. However, she's always had very loose stools, and I can't imagine how she could make the transition to a potty-chair. Do we need to wait until her stools are firmer before we tackle toilet training?

Answer: Absolutely not. The consistency of stools varies markedly for two-year-olds, and there is a wide range of normal. Also, remember that stools can appear more "smooshy" in diapers because they get sat on or otherwise squished. With toddlers, I see more problems with stools that are too firm than with ones that are too loose. Feel free to encourage your child's use of the potty.

Question: My daughter tends to get constipated for long periods of time. Even though she's almost three, I can't help but fear that toilet training will make this situation worse. Then we'll *really* have a problem on our hands! Any hints?

Answer: I think it's a good idea to work on the constipation issue first. Constipation is defined by the hardness of bowel movements, not by their infrequency. The best way to approach the problem is to make dietary changes. Try to increase your child's intake of water, and offer lots of "p" fruits (peaches, pears, prunes, and plums). Also, try to decrease your child's intake of binding foods such as rice, bananas, cheese, and applesauce. If that doesn't work, you may want to discuss other options with your pediatrician, including the use of laxatives. It can take several months to improve the situation if it's been going on for a long time. However, you probably won't need to delay toilet training during this time, as long as your child is showing signs of readiness.

Chapter 4
Get Ready

Now that your child seems ready for toilet training, it's time for you to get ready for the big adventure. Begin by gathering the materials and equipment you'll need for a successful and stress-free experience. There aren't a lot of supplies required, but the items you'll need are essential. Since there are plenty of choices out there, here's a guide to help you get ready.

Types of Toilets

There are three different types of toilets to choose from when you're beginning toilet training. Here are the potty picks and the pros and cons for each one.

Regular Adult Toilet

While the standard toilet may seem the most convenient way to train your child, most child development experts don't recommend it. The standard toilet is designed for an adult-size body. It's large, uncomfortable, and may be intimidating to a small child. Children often fear the loud flushing noise, the swirling water, and the mysterious objects that disappear into a seemingly black hole. Sitting on a big toilet can be scary for an unsteady child who can't touch the ground with his feet. A child may be afraid of falling off—or falling in.

Adult Toilet with an Adapter Seat

Adapter seats are designed to help a child sit safely and comfortably on an adult toilet. They come in a variety of styles to accommodate different preferences. The most common adapter seat is made of molded plastic shaped like a ring, with a smaller opening to help your child sit comfortably on the adult toilet. Most adapter seats are lightweight and portable, so you can take them with you when you travel or run errands. Some are inflatable, while others can be folded up, which makes them even more convenient.

When you use an adapter seat, there's no need for extra cleanup, since you simply flush the adult toilet. Once your child is comfortable on the adapter seat, you can eventually remove it and let your child make the transition to the adult toilet seat.

Some adults may consider certain adapter seats a nuisance, however, since they have to be removed for adult use and replaced for children's use. (Other adapter seats simply flip up to allow the adult to sit on the regular toilet seat.) Adapter seats can also be uncomfortable and unsteady, depending on the design, and they may come loose from the seat, causing the child to lose his balance and fall. If your child falls off the toilet seat, he may be reluctant to get back on.

To make the adapter seat more accessible, you may want to provide a stepstool or step-up ladder to help your child climb on more easily. A stepstool also gives your child leverage while he's sitting, and it's especially helpful for boys who prefer to stand while urinating.

Potty-Chair

Most children prefer the child-size potty-chair when beginning toilet training. Potty-chairs help make the experience less frightening, more pleasant, and a whole lot smoother. They're easier for children to use since they're the appropriate size. A child is naturally more comfortable sitting on a potty seat that's designed for his body.

In addition, a child usually feels safer using a potty-chair since he doesn't feel like he's going to fall off. A child can place his feet on the floor, which provides a sense of security and gives him better leverage for expelling bowel movements. Also, the potty-chair doesn't have any loud flushing noises or strange black holes that can frighten a child, and it can be moved from room to room for the convenience of both parents and children. Some potty-chairs are designed so they can be converted into stepstools when a child is ready to begin using an adult toilet. Other potty-chairs can be converted into adapter seats that can be placed on the adult toilet.

Quick Tip

I invested in two potty-chairs, one for the playroom and one for my kids' bedroom. This arrangement seemed to help my kids make it to the potty on time when they were learning. I also got one of those inflatable potty-chairs that you line with a plastic bag. I kept it in the car—since my girls were not equipped with a spout for easy peeing into a jar or onto the side of the road!

—Dana M.

Tips for Buying a Potty-Chair

Choosing the right potty-chair may seem overwhelming when you first begin your search. There are over a dozen different styles on the market, and they vary greatly. Here are some tips on what to look for.

Easy to Use

You want a potty-chair that will help develop your child's independence, self-esteem, and self-help skills. The more your child can do for himself, the better. Examine the potty-chair bowl and see if it's easy to remove so your child can dump the contents into the adult toilet without spilling. (Remember that spills sometimes occur no matter how easy the bowl is to remove.) Top removal is easier than back removal.

Child-Tested

Take your child shopping with you and let him help select the potty-chair. Let him try out different models, styles, and sizes to see how sturdy they are and how well they fit. Think about how the chair will fit your child as he grows.

Stable

Check to see if the chair remains stable when your child sits down, gets up, or leans over. Choose a chair that's lightweight enough to carry around your home, but sturdy enough to offer good support. Look for a broad base or strong legs so your child won't tip it over if he leans over or lands awkwardly while sitting down.

Comfortable

Make sure your child is comfortable on the potty, so he won't mind sitting there for several minutes. Make sure there are no sharp edges, sharp points, or areas that could pinch your child's skin. The best potty-chairs are smooth and molded from one piece of plastic.

Splatter Cup

Most potty-chairs include a splatter cup that helps guide the urine into the bowl. This is especially helpful for boys. Splatter cups are usually detachable, but they may not be comfortable if they're too wide, and they may not be useful if they're too loose or too narrow.

Seat Straps

Some potty-chairs come with seat straps to help secure your child while sitting. However, they may cause the chair to tip if your child leans over or stands up. Some children don't like the feeling of being tied down to the seat.

Armrests

Armrests can increase your child's comfort and leverage, but leaning on them may cause the chair to tip over. Check this out before buying the potty-chair.

More Than One

You might consider buying two potty-chairs, or more. Keep them in whatever rooms you plan to use for toilet training, such as the bathroom, your child's bedroom, the kitchen, the playroom, and so on. You might want to buy an inflatable toilet or adapter seat for taking with you on trips or when visiting family or friends.

Cost

Potty-chairs run anywhere from $10 to over $100, depending on the quality and the extras included. Think about your budget and the amenities that are important to you and your child.

Quick Tip

My child's pediatrician gave me the best advice: Buy a small plastic potty-chair and put it in the bathroom next to the toilet. It's messier because you have to clean it out, but your child will follow you into the bathroom, watch you, get the general idea, and train himself. It worked beautifully. At first, my son followed me in, pulled down his pants, sat down, and just chatted with me. The first time he tinkled I praised him and gave him a treat. Pretty soon he was using the potty-chair regularly with minimal accidents, and by two he was fully trained. The only downside was that he followed EVERYONE into the bathroom. We had some very startled guests.

—Rena L.

Toilet-Training Clothes

The clothes your child wears during this exciting time are crucial for helping him succeed. Here are the options and some things to consider.

Vinyl or Plastic Training Pants

The most popular clothing item for toilet training is pull-on training pants. They're easy to pull up and down, so your child can manage them by himself. Timing is important during this critical period, so you want your child's clothes to be easy for him to handle.

Pull-Up Diapers

Disposable pull-up diapers are designed like underpants. They're fairly easy for your child to pull up and down, and they provide the added convenience of containing urine or feces when your child has an accident. However, your child may not feel sufficiently uncomfortable after wetting a pull-up, which may reduce his motivation to use the toilet.

Cloth Underwear

These are made with layers of extra cotton to absorb urine or feces if your child has an accident. Unlike pull-ups, your child should feel wet and uncomfortable if he soils his underwear. However, they're not as absorbent as pull-ups, so you run the risk of having urine or feces escape into outer clothing and surrounding areas.

Some experts argue that you should make a clean break from diapers and avoid them altogether after training gets underway. They say that if a child doesn't feel the discomfort of wet pants, he won't be motivated to stay dry. You may want to start with cloth underwear and use pull-ups only after training is well established.

Larger Sizes

You may want to put your child in pants and underwear that are slightly larger than your child's current size, so they're easier to pull up and down. They should be loose at the waist, but not so loose that they keep falling down.

Nighttime Training Pants

Nighttime training pants are also available to help your child stay dry during the night, so he doesn't have to wear diapers.

Good Supply

It's best to have about eight to ten pairs of underpants and training pants available during the toilet-training process. Make sure you have lots of clean spares ready to go so you don't run out.

Big-Kid Underpants

When your child is ready for regular underpants, you might want to buy ones that are decorated with cartoon characters or special designs, to make wearing big-kid underpants even more fun. Let your child pick out his underpants so he has some control over the process.

Simple Design

Avoid clothes that have buckles, snaps, zippers, ties, buttons, belts, and other difficult fasteners. Also avoid tights, overalls, jumpsuits, and clothes that have to be tucked in, that are layered, or that are too long. Look for clothes with elastic waistbands, Velcro fasteners, and other features that make them easy to get on and off.

No Pants?

Weather permitting, you may choose to let your child go naked or wear a short shirt with no pants. If you have the nerve and the willingness to clean up, it's the easiest way to go!

Our son wanted to wear super-hero underpants and undershirts because he wanted to feel like Spider-Man or Batman. We told him that as soon as he could wear big-boy pants, he could wear the super-hero underpants. I'm proud to say he was potty trained before he entered high school.

—David K.

I kept the diapers on until my child used the potty a few times a day for a couple of days in a row. Then I took her shopping to pick out her underwear as a reward. She had some accidents at first, but she quickly learned to use the potty. Also, I gave her small rewards such as a candy or stickers or small toys when she went a full day without an accident. This extra incentive made all the difference.

—Kristin G.

From the moment I started potty training my child, I used regular underwear rather than pull-ups. For the first few days, I put plastic training pants over the regular underpants to avoid big messes.

—Becky G.

Other Materials and Equipment

Here are some other items you may want to have on hand when toilet training your child, to help make the experience more comfortable, pleasant, and fun.

Decorations

To make the potty-chair more inviting to your child (and to personalize it, too), add stickers and decals, or write your child's name on it with a permanent marker.

Toilet Paper

There are several ways to help your child learn how to measure the toilet paper when it's time to wipe. Some parents have their kids count off five squares of paper; others recommend having the child measure the paper along the length of his arm to determine the right amount. If the toilet paper dispenser is a short distance from the floor, you could have your child unroll the paper until it reaches the floor. If your child is having trouble controlling his desire to unravel the toilet paper, squeeze the roll a little to flatten the cardboard spool so it's harder to unroll. Some parents like to use special toddler wipes that can be flushed down the toilet.

Targets

Sometimes boys enjoy aiming their urine at targets floating in the toilet. You can buy tiny paper submarines made for this purpose, or you can make your own targets by cutting out small pieces of thin paper or newspaper comics and floating them in the toilet. Some parents sprinkle a handful of Cheerios in the water for boys to use as targets.

Food Coloring Fun

Pour a little water in the bottom of the potty-chair bowl. (This also makes cleanup easier.) Then add a few drops of blue food coloring. When your child's urine hits the water, it will turn green.

Lid

Some potty-chairs come with lids that cover the bowl when it's not in use. Some kids find lifting the lid fun and part of the ritual, but others find it a nuisance when they're in a hurry. Buy a potty-chair with a detachable lid in case your child doesn't like it.

Music

Some potty-chairs come with an attached music box that plays a tune when urine hits the bowl. Other potty-chairs play music the entire time the child is sitting on the potty. This can be relaxing and soothing, or it can be distracting, depending on the child. If you're not sure how your child will react, consider using a cassette or CD player to play music for your child while he's using the potty. If it becomes a problem or a distraction, remove it.

Books

Keep a supply of picture books nearby for your child to "read" or look at while sitting on the potty. This may help your child relax and sit for longer periods of time, if necessary. (See Appendix II.)

Toys

If your child prefers toys rather than books, keep a basketful within reach so he can entertain himself while sitting. Make sure the toys are easy to handle, and wash them periodically to keep them germfree.

Rewards

Some parents like to reward their children with small candies, crackers, or toys each time they're successful using the potty. Other parents use charts or stickers to mark successes as they happen, limiting toys or snacks to special occasions such as staying dry all day. Make sure you don't substitute candy and toys for praise. Your words of encouragement and approval are the most effective reward you can provide.

I put little red pieces of paper in the toilet for my boys to aim at. I even made a chart to keep track of how many pieces they sank.

—Melissa S.

I put a potty chart behind the door, bought a pack of stickers, and had my daughter place one sticker on the chart every time she went potty by herself. At the beginning, I gave her an extra reward with each sticker. After a while I gave her a reward after five stickers. Eventually I didn't need to give her a reward at all.

—Melissa S.

My friend Lori took her daughter to the store to select a big-girl potty. They ended up having to buy a traditional potty-chair that was kind of clinical looking. So Lori asked her daughter to pick out some hologram stickers to brighten it up, just like kids do with streamers on bicycle handles.

—Tracy O.

Bonus Tips for Toilet Time

Safe Place

If your child is frightened of the bathroom, you might begin toilet training in the kitchen or your child's bedroom, wherever he feels safe.

No Distractions

If your child is easily distracted, you might begin toilet training in a quiet room where he's more relaxed.

Company

If your child wants you to join him, feel free to do so. You could sit on the adult toilet while he sits on the potty-chair, or you could stand by while he takes care of business. Whatever makes him comfortable.

Extra Security

If your child feels insecure, hold his hand or talk to him while he uses the potty-chair or adult toilet.

Extra Clothing

Always have extra clothing on hand in case of accidents, especially if you're traveling, running errands, going to preschool, and so on.

Quick Tip

My friend told me that the potty-chair went wherever her daughter went during the toilet-training period. If they were in the kitchen, the potty-chair was next to the table. If they were watching a video, the potty-chair was next to the TV. She kept her daughter in a long shirt and loose pants (or none at all) so her daughter could use the potty on her own without Mom's help. Whenever her daughter got the urge, she just sat down on the nearby potty-chair. It was completely stress-free.

—Tracy O.

Dolls That "Wet"

Buy or borrow a doll that "takes" a bottle of water and then "wets." (See Appendix II.) Pick up a few accessories such as several baby bottles, some training pants, and some loose clothing.

Explain How It Works

When you give your child the doll, talk about what it can do (drink and urinate). Show him how it works, then let him play with it.

Play Together

Spend some time with your child playing with the doll and making up scenarios that involve the potty-chair.

"Train" the Doll

After you feed the doll a bottle of water, have your child go through the motions of training the doll how to use the toilet. Have him pull the doll's pants down and place the doll on the potty-chair.

Talk to the Doll

Chat with the doll (you and your child) while it's sitting on the potty-chair. Encourage the doll to urinate, then squeeze the doll to release the water.

Praise the Doll

After the doll "urinates," praise it for doing a good job, clap your hands, and tell the doll how proud you are of it.

Wipe the Doll

Let your child get a little toilet paper and wipe the doll, or have your child "teach" the doll how to wipe itself (always front to back). Throw the wet paper into the potty-chair or toilet.

Flush the Bowl

Have your child take the bowl to the big toilet and flush the contents, if he isn't afraid of the sound.

Redress the Doll

Once the doll is wiped and dry, put its clothes back on. Don't forget the underpants!

Wash Up

After the doll is dressed, have your child take it to the sink to wash its hands.

☺ Doll Play ✋

Doll play can be helpful in many ways, even to help sort out which equipment might be best for your child.

Sample Dialogue for Doll Play

While playing house with your child, you might encourage him to take Dolly or Teddy on a shopping trip. While you're "out," you could say, "Let's take a look at potty-chairs and big-boy pants while we're shopping! That way, when Dolly decides she's ready to use the potty, we'll have everything we need! Which type of potty-chair do you think she would like? The sit-down kind or the kind that goes on the big potty? What kind of big-girl pants do you think she would like? Ones with teddy bears or ones with hearts?" Make sure to use a tone that reflects your enthusiasm.

You can also suggest to your child that the best clothes for Dolly to wear are ones that are easy to get on and off, in case Dolly needs to go potty. You may even want to assemble Dolly's potty equipment, including diapers, "big-doll" pants, toilet paper, and books to read.

Ask Dr. Kelly

Question: As a pediatrician, do you have any recommendation on which type of toilet works best for toilet training?

Answer: In the majority of cases, children prefer the stability of the potty-chair. They like being able to put their feet on the floor, and they generally seem more comfortable. Children's needs vary, however, so don't hesitate to scope out other options, including adapter seats and adult toilets.

Question: Is it a bad idea to buy or borrow a secondhand potty-chair? Should I be concerned about diseases?

Answer: I think borrowing a used potty-chair or buying one at a consignment store is a great idea. One child isn't going to wear out a potty-chair, since it's used for only a short time. Spending less on the potty-chair will leave extra dollars for books, CDs, and other accessories. Plus, you may be more inclined to pick up an extra potty-chair or two if you don't have to pay full price. Give the potty-chair a thorough cleaning with a bleach-based solution, so you won't have to worry about germs, and make sure to rinse it thoroughly.

Question: I'm confused about using food to reward my child for potty successes. I've heard marvelous stories about M&Ms working great, but I've also heard that you shouldn't reward with food. What's your advice?

Answer: Some experts are concerned that rewarding with food, especially sweets, can lead to an unhealthy pattern of using food for positive reinforcement. Such habits could lead to overconsumption, which could lead to childhood obesity. Food should be viewed as an essential source of sustenance and nutrition. Personally, I believe this issue should be examined within each family's behavioral dynamic, with genetic predispositions taken into consideration. If treats are used, moderation is important.

Question: I want to make potty training as much fun as possible. What are some suggestions?

Answer: I agree that injecting fun and humor into the process can be enormously therapeutic, since it can reduce stress and provide needed relief in what can often be an intense undertaking for both parents and kids. Singing and dancing often lighten things up. Some people feel they also enhance the learning process. You may want to check out a musical potty-chair, or you may want to look at videos and CDs currently on the market. You could also put your creative juices to work by writing your own words to a favorite tune. For example, to "This is the way we wash our hands," you could sing, "This is the way we pee in the potty." You could also sing, "The pee in the potty goes flush, flush, flush" to the tune of "The Wheels on the Bus."

Chapter 5

Get Set

After you've gathered your toilet-training supplies, you're ready to take the next step. With a little preparation, planning, and practice, you'll be ready to guide your child when she shows signs of readiness.

Set the Stage

Like performers preparing for the stage, you and your child will be less stressed and more likely to succeed if you rehearse. If your child is well prepared, she'll be more comfortable and eager to learn this new skill.

Prepare Your Child

Talk to your child about the upcoming experience in a positive way. Talk about it in context, such as during diaper changing or when you're going to the bathroom. Tell her you're looking forward to working together on this new adventure and that she's going to be so proud of herself when she's accomplished this task. Ask your child questions to see if she understands, and listen to her carefully when she talks about her expectations (if she's able to do so). Be careful not to overhype the experience, however, or your child may become wary or resistant.

Share the Props

Show your child the props you'll be using for rehearsals and performances. Describe each piece of equipment, from the potty-chair to the training pants, and let your child explore everything at her own pace by touching it, sitting on it, and decorating it. Let her put the potty-chair wherever she wants (within reasonable limits), so she feels in control of it. Compare it to the adult toilet, and talk about the differences. Ask questions to make sure she understands your words, then see if she has any questions about the equipment.

Join Forces

Make sure everyone involved in toilet training your child understands the procedures to be followed, including your partner, your child's grandparents, siblings, babysitters, daycare providers, preschool teachers, and other people your child interacts with on a regular basis. Disagreements or misunderstandings among those involved will only confuse your child and may result in delays or disruptions. Although you'll likely be the primary trainer, you'll probably need others to help you and your child achieve this goal.

Use Books and Videos

Consider buying, renting, or checking out some toilet-training picture books and videos from the bookstore or library. (See Appendix II.) Review them first to make sure the content reinforces your methods. Before training begins, read the books and watch the videos with your child to let her see more clearly what's expected. Answer your child's questions or concerns as they come up. As training gets underway, reread the books and watch the videos again to reinforce the message.

State Your Expectations

While you're chatting with your child about toilet training, let her know exactly what's going to happen step by step. Go over the process several times so it's clear in her mind. Tell her what her role will be so she understands that *she* will be in control of the process. Let her know what your role will be, too, but keep it minimal so your child sees this as *her* adventure. Be sure to explain the benefits of using the toilet:

- No more diapers
- No more uncomfortable wetness or odor
- No more changing table
- Getting to wear big-boy/big-girl pants
- Being like the big kids
- Getting to use the potty-chair (and eventually the big toilet)
- Being dry and comfortable all the time
- Getting to use the bathroom like grownups do
- Getting to go to preschool

Play Show and Tell

Set an example by showing your child how to use the toilet. Leave the door open and let her see you, or invite her in if she's interested. Let your child sit on her potty-chair while you sit on the big toilet. Don't make a big deal of it. It's best to remain casual and nonchalant so your child will feel the same way. If you're doing most of the training, make sure your partner gets a chance to offer his or her perspective as well. Explain each step as you go about your business, including:

- Noticing that you have to go to the bathroom
- Pulling down your pants and underpants
- Sitting on the toilet (or standing in front of it)
- Urinating or defecating
- Tearing off some toilet paper
- Wiping from front to back
- Getting off the toilet seat
- Pulling up your pants
- Flushing the toilet
- Washing your hands

Quick Tips

I brought out the potty-chair and let my child take it apart, put it together, drag it from room to room, and sit on it while watching a video about going potty. Once he became comfortable with the potty-chair and showed signs that he was ready to use it, I cancelled all my scheduled events for a week. I let him run around naked, reminding him periodically where pee-pee and poop go. By the third day, we were basically done except for a few minor accidents—and stains on the carpet.

—Kristy D.

I was used to taking my child with me to the bathroom. It was a good way to keep an eye on him while I used the toilet. When I felt he was ready to begin toilet training, I started talking about the process so he could take more notice of what was going on. Seeing me go all the time (and my husband, too, but not as much) really helped when it came time for him to try.

—Melanie E.

Observe Your Child

Watch for early signs that your child needs to use the toilet. Common signs include appearing to be distracted, dancing around, holding her genital area, seeming to be anxious, or saying something about being wet or uncomfortable. When you see any of these signs, ask your child if she has to use the toilet (or if she has just filled her diaper).

Create a Plan

While gathering information about your child's elimination habits, read the next chapter so you'll know what to do during the training process. Go over the steps several times to create a clear mental guideline. If you need prompts, photocopy or tear out the sheets from Appendix I and post them in the potty room(s) for easy reference.

Record a Timetable

You may want to create a chart that documents your child's elimination habits. Some children are very regular, while others are more difficult to anticipate. Keep track of how often (and what time) your child urinates and defecates, and make notes of any signs your child exhibits prior to soiling her diaper. Record the details, and see if you can determine a pattern of timing and behavior.

Find the Right Time

Selecting the right time for toilet training is crucial to success. Not only do you want to be sure your child is physically, cognitively, and emotionally ready, you want to choose the best calendar time possible (after your child demonstrates readiness, of course).

Season

Many parents say summer is best, since a child doesn't need to wear many clothes, if anything at all (weather permitting). The fewer the clothes, the easier it is for a child to use the toilet. Others say winter isn't so bad because long pants tend to absorb urine when a child has an accident, reducing the risk of stains to carpeting and furniture.

At-Home Vacation

You might want to plan an at-home vacation and use the time for toilet training. This may help you feel more relaxed, less stressed, and may allow you to avoid disruptions that could delay the process. If you're planning to travel while on vacation, you should probably delay toilet training until you get back home. Life is too distracting when you're away from home, and distractions can impede the process.

Long Weekend

If you don't have much vacation time to use, consider training your child on a weekend, especially if you have a long weekend coming up. Plan to devote the entire time to toilet training with as few interruptions as possible.

Time of Day

For some children, morning is the best time to begin toilet training, so they can start the day with that goal in mind. Other kids do better in the afternoon, after they've had a chance to ease into the day. If you have a sense of when your child will respond favorably, go for that time. If your selection isn't working, try another time and see if you get a better response.

Schedule

Sometimes a child's elimination schedule determines the toilet-training schedule. Many children need to use the toilet after mealtime; others need to go first thing in the morning or after nap time.

Quick Tip

I was lucky that my kids were ready to train in the summer. It was SO much easier. I let them walk around pantless and waited til they had to go. If your child happens to be ready during the colder months, you can always turn up the heat and pretend it's warm outside.

—Barbara S.

Rehearse the Play

Once you and your child are prepped and psyched for toilet training, it's time to rehearse the play. Here are some tips to help your child go through the motions so she's ready for the actual performance.

Two's Company?

Some children want parents to accompany them to the toilet. They need the extra security of having them around in case something happens. Other kids show signs of modesty and prefer to use the toilet alone. It's better if you join your child, so you can encourage her and make sure she doesn't have problems. But if she insists on going alone, tell her to keep the door open so you can keep an eye on her.

Quick Response

Take a few minutes each day to practice a quick response to needing to use the toilet. Talk about the sensations of having to go, then pretend it's time to go. For example, you might say, "Do you have to go pee-pee?" or, "Do you have to go poo-poo?" or, "Do you think it's time to sit on the potty?" Have your child practice hurrying to the potty-chair, pulling her pants down, and sitting on the toilet. Applaud each successful rehearsal.

Positive Reinforcement

Before you officially start the session, check your child from time to time, and praise her if she's still dry. If she's wet, let her know, in case she's not fully aware of the feeling. Then talk about how she's almost ready to use the toilet.

Name the Body Parts

At bath time or changing time, make a game of naming the appropriate body parts for toilet training, including your child's genitals, so she understands the terms and feels comfortable using them. You should be clear and honest about the words used for body parts and toileting behavior, but there's no reason why you couldn't use simpler terms that are easier for your child to say, such as *pee-pee* and *poo-poo* instead of *urinate* and *defecate*.

Include the Potty Naturally

Leave the potty-chair in the bathroom or the room where you're planning to train your child, so she can get used to seeing it. Mention it from time to time, but don't overdo it, so your child doesn't feel pressured. Let your child check out other toilets in people's homes and in public places, so she sees they're everywhere!

Do Some Relaxation Techniques

Teach your child some relaxation techniques to help her be more aware of her body and sensitive to the signs of having to use the toilet. Have her lie down on the floor, then encourage her to relax each part of her body as you name it. Then teach her how to tighten and release the body part by squeezing it and letting it go. Start with her fist, then move to her arm, neck, tummy, leg, and so on.

Avoid Distractions

Keep distractions to a minimum during toilet-training sessions. Choose a quiet time, at home, when no friends or other visitors are around.

Use a Doll

Let your child play with a doll (preferably one that feeds and wets) before you start a training session. Let her feed the doll, dress it, take it to the potty, have it urinate, and clean up after it.

Quick Tip

Our younger daughter dragged on and on, and I thought she'd never be toilet trained. So I found an old Betsy Wetsy doll, filled up a water bottle, took off my daughter's clothes, and brought the potty-chair into the kitchen. I told her it would be fun to train the doll to use the potty, so we set the doll on the potty and gave it some water. We waited a minute, then checked to see if the doll "went." Then we clapped for the doll and gave it a goody. My daughter ate the goody, took the bowl to the toilet, poured the water in, and flushed. We yelled, "Bye-bye, pee-pee!" Then I said, "Let's show the doll how YOU go pee-pee." My daughter sat down on the potty, drank some apple juice, and went! We cheered, she got a goody, and she flushed the pee-pee bye-bye! After a while, the goody wasn't even a priority. Our shared excitement was reward enough.

—Julie L.

Doll Play

You can use doll play during rehearsal time to assess your child's readiness for toilet training.

Sample Dialogue for Doll Play

While sitting with your child and her teddy bear on the floor, you could ask your child, "Do you think it's a good idea to ask Teddy if he's ready to go potty? Won't it be exciting when Teddy thinks he's ready to use the potty-chair? We'll have to make sure we have some treats ready in case he's able to put pee-pee in the potty! What kinds of treats do you think Teddy would like?" If your child is reluctant to talk about the subject, you should back off for a while. Later, you might ask, "When do you think Teddy might be ready? When summertime comes and we're wearing shorts and bathing suits a lot?"

Ask Dr. Kelly

Question: When it came time to wean our daughter from the pacifier, a friend gave us a marvelous tip. She recommended throwing out the pacifiers and reporting to our child that the "binky fairy" had come to take them away and bring them to younger babies. It worked so well we thought the same strategy would work for toilet training. Unfortunately, the "diaper fairy" didn't come through. Instead, we had a series of accidents and a very upset little girl. Why didn't it work?

Answer: *You* may have been ready to have your daughter trained, but she wasn't ready. The strategy is clever, but the timing needs to be right. Only when your child shows the proper signs of readiness, including wanting to master the toilet, should you begin reinforcing her desire with fun games like visits from the diaper fairy. In addition to having the fairy remove the baby item, have her replace it with a book or some other big-girl item. This will provide an added incentive for your child and will set the stage for the tooth fairy's first visit.

Question: My friend told me she had a great tip that was certain to make toilet training fast and easy. Apparently, when her son was visiting his grandparents' house, his grandfather took him by the hand and said, "Let's go outside. I want to show you how we can pee on a rock." In the privacy of their backyard, the grandfather demonstrated how this was done. The boy was awestruck and followed the example without hesitation. My friend told me he never had an accident after that! I wasn't sure what to think of this, but when my husband tried it with our son, he looked at us like we were crazy! What do you think?

Answer: I hear many stories in which an "exactly right" action, phrase, or circumstance triggers toilet mastery almost immediately. These stories are fun to tell, but in reality I think the circumstances are more coincidental than causal. This particular child was probably ready for toilet training. When the grandfather added a game-like component with a fun twist, it probably encouraged success in a child who was ready to take off on his own.

Question: We talked with our 18-month-old about using the potty, but we didn't pressure her to do so. When she finally showed signs of interest, we went out and bought a pack of training pants. But when we tried to put them on, she didn't want anything to do with them! Did we miss a critical window of opportunity?

Answer: Absolutely not! Fleeting interest and true readiness are not the same thing. There is no limited time frame in which a child will be ready to be toilet trained. Once your child is truly ready, she will remain ready.

Question: When our son turned two, we made a special trip to the store to let him pick out his potty-chair. He seemed so excited, but now that the chair is out of the box and into the bathroom, he seems reluctant to sit on it. Does this mean he isn't ready?

Answer: Some children like to practice sitting on the potty-chair with their clothes on, just to get a feel for it. You might use this as a way of assessing your son's readiness. If he remains defiant, you should delay toilet training. Leave the potty-chair out where he can see it, and tell him there will come a time when he feels more comfortable using it. In the meantime, look for other signs of readiness, and wait until the time is right.

Chapter 6

Go!

After all that planning and preparation, it's finally time to *go!* So, with a positive attitude, the right props, and some potty prompts, you're ready for this exciting, life-changing event. Just remember to stay relaxed, upbeat, and optimistic, and soon your child will be out of diapers forever!

Take the First Steps

In order to learn to walk, your child had to take those first steps. Once he got the hang of it, there was no stopping him. It's the same with toilet training. Help your child take those first steps, and watch how quickly he progresses. Remind yourself that this is just another teaching opportunity, although it may seem more difficult at times. Try to maintain the same attitude you have when you're teaching your child any other task.

Choose a Free Day

Select a day when you have nothing else planned—no play groups, no errands, no babysitter, no illnesses, no stresses. With no distractions, you and your child can better focus on the task.

Dress Your Child in Transition Pants

Begin the process by changing your child into transition pants—either pull-up diapers or training pants. Let him dress himself (if he's interested) and practice pulling his pants up and down. Talk to your child about why he's wearing these new clothes and how exciting it is to dress like a big kid.

Watch for Signs

Keep a close eye on your child so you can watch for signs that he needs to use the potty (feeling distracted, dancing around, holding his genitals). Remind him of these signs so he'll learn to associate them with the physical sensation of needing to go potty. When he shows one or more of these signs, escort him to the potty as calmly and quickly as possible. Don't panic! It's not a life-or-death situation.

Follow Your Child's Schedule

Some children's elimination habits are so regular, you can practically set your watch by them. If your child urinates or defecates at predictable times each day, anticipate these by heading toward the potty-chair. Tell your child you think it's time for him to use the toilet, then have him sit down and give it a try.

Motivate Your Child

If your child is reluctant to try the potty-chair, you might want to provide motivational rewards for each step taken toward that goal. For example, you might give him a sticker if he pulls down his own pants, or you might try a treat if he sits on the toilet for a few minutes.

Chart the Progress

Many parents have great success motivating their children by monitoring their progress on a chart. Children often need concrete visual reminders to help them understand abstract concepts, such as learning to use the toilet. Here's a simple way to construct and use a toilet-training chart:

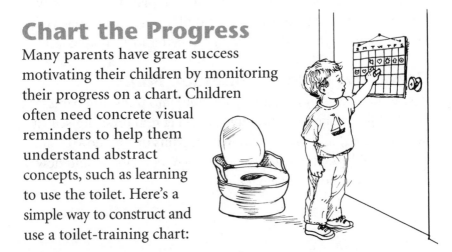

1. Buy a large sheet of poster board in your child's favorite color.

2. Draw a calendar-type grid with seven squares across and five squares down, leaving room at the top and left side. Leave plenty of space in each square for stickers, drawings, comments, and so on.

3. At the very top, write the title of the chart (for example, "Luke's Potty Chart"). Make the title big and beautiful!

4. Write the names of the days of the week across the top squares (under the title), and write the number of the weeks down the left side.

5. Post the chart in your child's room or in the bathroom where he'll see it often. It will serve as both a progress chart and a motivational reminder to use the toilet.

6. Each time your child uses the toilet, give him a star or sticker to put on the chart. Or let him draw a mark in the appropriate square. He'll be delighted to see the squares fill up with stars, stickers, or marks.

7. At the end of each day, discuss your child's progress enthusiastically and give him a special treat, if you like.

Quick Tip

I kept a bag of chocolate kisses on top of the fridge, and every time my son used the toilet, he got one. The training process was also helped along by the fact that he didn't like the feeling of poop in his pants. Plus, he very much wanted to be a "big boy." He was trained by age two.

—Susan W.

Stay on Course

Praise the Progress

Praise is the most effective motivator you can use with your child. Your smiling face, clapping hands, and proud words will help your child make steady progress using the toilet. Be sure to say something positive each time your child makes an effort to use the potty, and let him know how much progress he's making as he moves along. Here are some examples of positive statements you might use:

- "What a good job!"
- "You should be proud of yourself!"
- "You got to the toilet fast that time!"
- "I like the way you use only a few sheets of toilet paper!"
- "You're such as big boy/girl!"
- "I bet that felt good!"
- "You're really good at sitting on the toilet!"
- "You're such a fast learner!"

Use Potty Prompts

Don't forget to use potty prompts throughout the toilet-training sessions. Remind your child to go to the potty every so often, or ask him if he feels he needs to go. Have him check himself to see if he's still dry, and mention the reward you've planned the next time he uses the potty. Here are some positive potty prompts you might try:

- "Do you feel like you have to use the potty?"
- "Do you want to try the toilet now?"
- "Should we go sit on the potty and see if you have to go?"
- "Do you think you have to pee or poop?"
- "Are you still dry?"
- "Should we give the toilet another try?"

Go to the Bathroom Together

You might want to go to the toilet together with your child in the beginning, to make it more fun and less frightening for him. Each time your child sits on the potty-chair, sit on the toilet or chair nearby and chat or read a book with him. Whenever you have to use the toilet, tell your child you have to go, and tell him he's welcome to come along and try out his potty-chair. If you're pretty sure your child needs to go but he's reluctant to do so, tell him you need to go, then ask him if he wants to go first or second. Letting him decide might be all the motivation he needs.

To Flush or Not to Flush

If your child is using the adult toilet, ask him if he wants to flush it himself—and let *him* decide. Some kids enjoy having control over the toilet. The swirling water can be fascinating, and its disappearance can be magical. If the noise is too loud or scary for your child, wait until he's out of the room before flushing. Or tell him to plug his ears so he can see the swirling water but not hear the loud noise. If your child is using the potty-chair, have him help you remove the bowl and dump the waste into the adult toilet. Then have him flush or not, whichever he prefers.

Quick Tip

My son refused to pee in the toilet. He would only go on the grass in our backyard. So I bought a bag of suckers and put them in a jar. Then I put the jar on top of the toilet tank. I told him, "Every time you go pee-pee in the potty, you can have a sucker at the end of the day." The suckers were soon gone, and he always went in the potty after that.

—Debbie A.

Follow Through

Now that you've officially started the lesson, it's important to follow through with continued prompts, practice, praise, and rewards.

Make Frequent Visits

Try to have your child sit on the potty-chair once every hour or so. Sitting on the potty-chair may become a trigger that helps your child release his bladder and bowels.

Offer Reminders

Your child may become so engaged in play that he may disregard the need to go or may forget to use the potty. Remind him often, but don't overdo it. Constant interruptions and reminders may lead to a power struggle.

Expect Accidents

It takes time to learn a new task, especially at a young age. *There will be accidents,* so take them in stride. Don't make a big deal about them, or your child may become inhibited or feel like a failure. If your child has an accident, make a nonjudgmental comment (see the examples below), clean up the mess (let him help if he wants), and move on. Here are some things to say if your child has an accident:

- "It's okay! Accidents happen."
- "Everyone has accidents now and then—even Superman!"
- "I used to have accidents when I was first learning how to the use the toilet."
- "Don't worry. You'll do better next time."
- "You were having so much fun today, your probably just forgot."
- "No big deal. Let's change you clothes, and you can try again later."
- "Try to listen to your body more carefully, and you'll make it next time."
- "You almost made it that time! Good job!"

Continue Praising and Rewarding

Don't let up on the positive reinforcement. Keep telling your child that he's doing a good job and you're proud of him. If he needs rewards in addition to praise, try some stickers, small treats, or a progress chart. Or offer a special reward at the end of the day or week.

Quick Tip

For our older daughter, we kept a stash of stickers in the bathroom, and she would get a small handful for going to the potty. She liked decorating her clothes and toys with them. I would sit across from her on the edge of the bathtub and read to her while she sat on the potty. She was fully trained right around her third birthday.

—Julie L.

Gender Differences

Although boys and girls generally show the same signs of readiness, there are some general differences in how and when they toilet train. (Individual boys and girls may vary from the following tendencies.)

Girls

- Are usually ready to train at 30–36 months.
- Often learn faster than boys, unless they're not really ready.
- Use only the sitting position.
- Have women as role models more often than men.
- Are usually more sensitive than boys to their bodies' signals.

Boys

- Are usually ready to train at 36–42 months.
- Often take longer to train, unless they're ready, in which case they learn very quickly.

- Use either a sitting or standing position for urinating. (Some boys have trouble aiming and directing their urine flow when they're learning. You may want to start them in the sitting position, then have them switch to the standing position when they're ready. You may want to put targets in the toilet.)
- Also have women as role models more often than men.
- Are generally more physically active than girls and less aware that they have to use the potty.

☺ Doll Play ✋

A perfect way to take the pressure off your child and still teach the principles of using the toilet is involving your child's favorite doll or teddy in some imaginary play. You may want to consider buying or borrowing a doll specifically designed for this purpose.

Sample Dialogue for Doll Play

While playing house with your child and his doll or teddy bear, you might say to your child, "Dolly told me she wants to wear big-girl pants today, not a diaper. She asked me to remind her to go pee-pee in her potty-chair. Do you know what might be a fun idea? Let's make a sticker chart for Dolly and have her put a sticker on it if she keeps her big-girl pants dry the whole time we play house! And she can get another sticker each time she tinkles in the potty-chair! When she gets five stickers, we can all go out for a special treat! I can hardly wait!"

Ask Dr. Kelly

Question: I hear so many stories about offering rewards to children for successful toileting—everything from toy cars to a whole train set! I thought bribery was bad!

Answer: There's a fine line between positive reinforcement and bribery. You might seek your child's input and ask if there's something special (within reason, of course) he'd like to have once he's learned to use the potty. I would discourage rewarding with things you've already decided are off-limits, such as candy, soda, violent toys, staying up late, and so on. Instead, choose an appropriate reward *together with your child,* and make sure you have something that will be available when the time comes.

Question: Should hand washing be part of the training process?

Answer: I think personal hygiene is an important part of toilet training, and I encourage parents to be good examples for their children and show them how to wash their hands.

Question: Is it wrong to pick a target date for the completion of toilet training?

Answer: A specific date may not be realistic, but in the context of encouraging your child and communicating your enthusiasm, you could say something like, "I wonder if you'll be wearing big-boy pants by the time your third birthday comes!" or, "I wouldn't be surprised if you're using the potty by the time you're Johnny's age (the boy next door)!" These are specific ways to show your child how excited you are about his toileting success without putting too much pressure on him.

Question: I've heard conflicting advice about whether or not you should avoid diapers altogether once you've put your child in training pants. What should I do?

Answer: I think this depends on the particular situation, and I think the child should often be a partner in this decision. Even though it may seem like a step back, you can view returning to diapers as an appropriate way to give your child support and to communicate that readiness is in your *child's* hands, not yours. If your child wants to go back to diapers, you might consider using ones that are a size smaller, so your child feels slightly uncomfortable. Perhaps your child will decide to move on to big-kid pants after all!

Chapter 7
Keep Going

Although you've accomplished a lot with your child, the lessons aren't over yet. You'll want to continue monitoring your child's elimination habits and reinforcing everything she's learned. Here are some tips for helping her solidify her developing skills.

Ask

Ask your child every hour or so if she needs to use the potty. If she starts getting annoyed by these questions, reduce their frequency or choose another strategy.

Remind

You may want to simply remind your child occasionally to use the potty when she needs to. She may be ready to take control of the timing.

Suggest

If it's been a while since your child used the toilet (a couple of hours, for example), you might suggest she give it a try.

Praise

Continue to praise your child for each success. You may even want to praise her when she's not actually using the potty, to provide a subtle reminder. Give your child additional rewards as needed, if you've been using them. Over time, you should be able to eliminate special rewards and rely on praise alone.

Make It Fun

You can make the toilet-training experience even more pleasant by incorporating fun and games at toilet time. Here are some ways to reinforce what your child has learned.

Doll Play

Engage in imaginary play with your child and her teddy bear or doll (preferably one that wets), and provide some accessories to enhance the play. (See "Doll Play" sections throughout this book.)

Word Games

Play word games with your child while she's sitting on the toilet. Here are some examples:

- To play "I Spy," look around the room, identify an object, describe a characteristic of the object, and have your child try to guess what it is. For example, you might say, "I spy something white." Your child might say, "Toilet!"

- To play "Twenty Questions," think of something your child understands, and have your child try to guess the object by asking yes-no questions (no more than twenty).

- To play "Rhyme Time," say a word, and have your child say another word that rhymes with it. For example, you might say, "Flush," and your child might say, "Mush."

- To play "Opposites," say a word (such as "hot") and have your child say the opposite word ("cold").

- To play "Create a Story," take turns telling a story with your child. Say a sentence or two, and have your child continue the story. Go back and forth until you decide the story is finished.

Books

Read age-appropriate books to your child, including ones about using the toilet. (See Appendix II.)

Songs

Sing songs with your child, or play musical tapes or CDs and sing along.

Color Fun

Add blue food coloring to the potty water so your child can see it turn green when she urinates.

Conversation

Talk about anything and everything. This is a great opportunity to enjoy quality time together.

Quick Tips

I toilet trained my child with a little help from the "potty fairy." I told my daughter that the potty fairy left jellybeans in a special container in the bathroom. Whenever she used the potty, she got a prize from the potty fairy. The potty fairy gave one jellybean for pee-pee and three jellybeans for poopie. It worked beautifully. The bathroom became a place my child wanted to visit on a regular basis. I was also amazed at how quickly she learned to count.
—Kelly S.

I put up pictures in our bathroom of boys and girls using the potty. Seeing others use the toilet helped motivate my child to learn.
—Melissa S.

Follow-Up Tips

Here are some toilet-training tips to consider during the follow-up period.

Toilet Paper

Remind your child how much toilet paper to use, such as an arm's length, four to six squares, or until the paper reaches the floor.

Wiping

Make sure your child wipes from front to back so she doesn't introduce infection into her genital area.

Toilet Paper Only

Let your child know that *only* toilet paper goes in the toilet. Tell her if she puts toys or other objects in the toilet, it may get clogged up and overflow.

Flushing Fascination

Talk about what happens after flushing, if your child is interested. Describe how urine and feces go down the pipes and into the sewer (or wherever they go). Also talk about where the water comes from, what causes the flushing, and so on. Many children find these details fascinating.

Fun Soap

Try to find bars of soaps in fun colors or with cartoon designs or creative shapes on them, or use liquid soap dispensers that have fun designs on them.

Stepstool

It's a good idea to have a stepstool in each bathroom, so your child can turn the light switch on and off, climb onto the adult toilet when she's ready, and reach the sink to wash her hands.

What to Watch For

Here are some tips for the child who is reluctant to continue toilet training.

Potty Fears

Watch for fears that your child may be afraid to use the potty or toilet.

Elimination Fears

Watch for fears that your child is afraid to urinate or defecate.

Distractions

Watch for events that are going on in your child's world that may cause her to be reluctant to use the toilet, such as a new baby in the house, a move to a new house, and so on.

Negativity

Be prepared for some resistance and negativity if your child is going through what some call the "terrible twos."

Doctor Checkup

Have your pediatrician check for any physical problems that may be interfering with toilet training. Constipation, in particular, may be a significant obstacle.

Switching to the Big Toilet

If your child was trained on the potty-chair, she'll eventually want to try the big toilet. She may be afraid at first, or she may be so eager she makes mistakes. You may find that your child's ability to use the big toilet may come in handy at times, especially when you're out and about and the potty-chair isn't available. If she's ready to try, here are some ways to help her take that final step.

Make Sure She's Ready

Some children seem eager to use the big toilet, but they really aren't ready. If your child is managing her clothing easily, using the potty-chair well, and not having many accidents, she's probably ready. If she still needs practice with these skills, give her a little more time before trying the big toilet. If she's afraid of the size or the noise, don't push it.

Talk About the Big Toilet

Have a chat about the big toilet before you have your child take that first step toward switching. This will help plant the idea in your child's mind and prepare her psychologically for the change. Discuss how the big toilet is similar to, yet different from the potty-chair, and why grownups like to use it. Feel free to show her different kinds of toilets (including urinals) when you're out and about.

Get a Stepstool

Buy a small stepstool or two to help your child reach the big toilet. They also come in handy for reaching the sink. Let your child play a role in choosing the right one. Then decorate it with stickers, or write you child's name on it using a permanent marker. Have your child practice stepping up and down on the stepstool while holding the toilet seat.

Consider an Adapter Seat

You may want to use an adapter seat the first few times your child tries the big toilet, to make her feel more secure. Some children prefer this, while others prefer to use the actual toilet seat. Let your child make the decision.

Practice

Have your child sit on the big toilet without pulling her pants down, to let her get a feel for what it's like. The big toilet is less likely to be intimidating if your child gets a chance to test it without any pressure or expectations.

Have Your Child Give It a Try

When you think your child is ready to try the big toilet, tell her she can use it the next time she needs to go. Discourage this attempt if your child is in a hurry, so she can have plenty of time to make the adjustment without having an accident.

The Big Switch

Soon your child will choose the big toilet over the potty-chair, since it will make her feel more grown-up. Keep the potty-chair on hand for nighttime visits, emergencies, or temporary regressions.

We used to sit with our daughter in the bathroom while she was learning to use the big toilet. Praise was quite effective with her...so effective, in fact, that when I took her with me to the hardware store, she often wanted to sit on the display toilets—and she usually expected lots of positive feedback.

—David K.

Doll Play

Your child's teddy bear or doll (and indirectly your child) will surely want to be praised for successful pottying and for making the transition to the big toilet. Doll play is often a good way to reinforce the message without overstating the point.

Sample Dialogue for Doll Play

During imaginary play with your child and her teddy bear, you might say to your child, "Isn't it wonderful that Teddy has been wearing big-boy pants ever since his birthday, and that he only uses a diaper at night? Teddy has also learned to ride a tricycle and build a house with blocks! Wow! He's sure getting to be a big teddy bear! We are so proud of you, Teddy!"

At another opportunity, you might say, "Teddy, how about trying to use the same potty Mommy Teddy and Daddy Teddy use? You can also try flushing the toilet all by yourself! You can say bye-bye to pee-pee and poopie after you flush! Let's give it a try!"

Ask Dr. Kelly

Question: I get so frustrated when I dress my two-year-old in a new pair of big-boy underwear, and he poops in them, seemingly in defiance and despite my admonitions. Someone said I should make my son hand wash his underpants to teach him a lesson. Is this a good idea?

Answer: I'd advise against it. Laundering clothes is not an appropriate responsibility for a two-year-old. If your child doesn't seem to have a clue about when he's urinating or defecating, or if he seems to have "accidents" just to defy you, then he probably isn't ready to train. On the other hand, if he seems truly interested and is showing signs of readiness, you might encourage him to stick with it despite the accidents. Tell him it's okay that he didn't get to the potty-chair in time, and that you're confident he'll be able to do it next time. My personal preference is never to involve a child in cleaning up soiled clothing or bedding.

Question: My nearly three-year-old daughter has excellent control of her bladder. She even stays dry overnight. But when she needs to poop, she often disappears into a closet or behind a curtain. It's almost as if she's ashamed of herself! How should I handle this?

Answer: Such "hiding" behavior is not unusual during toilet training. We don't completely understand why it happens, but rest assured that the final stage of toilet mastery is not far off. I've heard stories of children asking their parents for a diaper and then trekking off to a private area to poop. Take it in stride, try to have a sense of humor about it, and make sure you don't shame, berate, or laugh at your child. It will pass.

Question: War has been declared in our home! My wife and I understand that our two-year-old son is going through an independence stage, but his defiance is almost overwhelming! Yesterday, we watched him deliberately pee and poop in his big-boy pants, and later on he spit out the beans we made him try! We're afraid to take him anywhere! Help!

Answer: Parents occasionally need to be reminded that they don't have the ability to force their children to eat, void, defecate, or fall asleep on command. Toddlers are keenly aware of this, and consequently huge battles can ensue if parents push too hard. These battles are not only unpleasant, but unproductive. As far as feeding is concerned, you should make nutritious foods available to your child at regular intervals, and let him be in charge of the kinds and amounts of food he eats. With regard to toilet training, make it clear to your child that he will learn to use the toilet when he's ready and interested. In the meantime, back off for a while, and avoid unnecessary confrontations.

Question: My 28-month-old daughter made the transition from diapers to the potty-chair quite smoothly. She's also night trained. However, we had a run of busy days recently, and I realized she was urinating only two or three times a day! Sometimes she doesn't urinate in the morning until she's been up for several hours. I'm concerned she isn't emptying her bladder often enough. Is this a problem?

Answer: If your daughter is eating well, drinking well, and producing regular bowel movements, there's nothing to worry about. Some children prefer emptying their bladders less frequently.

Chapter 8
Troubleshooting

While toilet training goes smoothly for most children, some encounter problems that delay or interfere with the process. Here are some typical toilet-training concerns and how to deal with them.

Staying Dry

If your child has trouble staying dry, you might need to check him more frequently and remind him to use the toilet.

Power Struggle

If your child seems to be in a power struggle with you, have someone else do the training for a while, such as your partner, a grandparent, or a babysitter. Or back off for a few weeks.

Bad Location

If your child doesn't like the room where the potty-chair is located, try moving it to a new room or hallway.

Insufficient Motivation

If your child doesn't seem sufficiently motivated, you might try to increase his rewards for pottying success. You can wean him from the rewards over time. If you're using pull-ups only, your child may not be feeling sufficiently uncomfortable—and therefore may not be sufficiently motivated to stay dry. Consider switching to cloth training pants so your child can feel the discomfort of wetness and hopefully be motivated to avoid it.

Stiff Resistance

If your child continues to resist toilet training, he may not be ready. Take a break for a while, and try again when he shows more interest. Don't get angry; this adds unnecessary stress and makes training more difficult.

Difficult Personality

If your child is unusually difficult or defiant, you might try giving him choices. For example, you might say, "Do you want to try the potty before lunch or after lunch?" or, "Do you want to sit on the little potty or the big potty?" or, "Do you want to go first or do you want Mommy to go first?"

Contrariness

You might try reverse psychology on your child (saying the opposite of what you'd normally say). For example, instead of saying, "Do you want to use the potty?" you might say, "You don't want to use *this* potty, do you?"

Inappropriate Time

If your child seems distracted because there's too much going on in his life (feeling ill, family vacation, moving day, new baby, new daycare situation, recent divorce, and so on), then you may want to back off for a while.

Not Drinking Enough

If your child doesn't seem to have to go very often, you might want to try increasing his fluid intake, at least during the training period. If he seems to have to go often and is having accidents, you might want to reduce his fluid intake. Talk to your doctor first.

Unwilling to Get Out of Bed

If your child is reluctant to use the potty during the night because he has to get out of bed or because he has to leave his room, you might want to put the potty-chair next to his bed so it's more convenient.

Babysitters and Daycare

If you use a babysitter or daycare provider, you'll want to tell the provider you're going through the toilet-training process so you can get your signals straight. Let your provider know what techniques you're using, what you want her to do, and how you'd like her to deal with accidents and other problems. You may want to buy her a copy of this book, or jot down key points you'd like her to follow. The checklists in Appendix I might also be helpful.

Deliberate Mishaps

If your child seems to urinate or defecate away from the potty on purpose, don't overreact and turn it into a power struggle. Just help your child change his pants and clean up the mess, and give him the attention he needs.

Holding BMs

If your child seems to be holding back his bowel movements, offer him more liquids, a high-fiber diet, and some fruit. While he's on the toilet, have him do some relaxation techniques (page 60), read a book, or listen to music. Always check with your doctor before trying laxatives or other remedies for constipation.

Accidents

If your child is having frequent accidents, especially in the beginning, don't make a big deal out of it. Accidents are a normal part of the training process. Just change your child into fresh training pants, clean up the mess, and keep going. Don't forget to offer lots of reminders and encouragement.

I heard that you should NEVER put children back in diapers after they've switched to training pants. I followed this advice, and luckily it worked for my children. However, some parents I've talked to said it didn't work for them. It's probably best to wait until things get really bad before you switch back to diapers.

—Dana M.

Travel Tips

If you're on the road a lot with your child, or if you have to make a long trip together, you'll want to prepare so you can keep the toilet-training program running smoothly.

Go Before You Go

Have your child use the potty before you leave, so he's less likely to have to go when you're driving down the road.

Bring Along a Porta-Potty

If you think your child will need a familiar seat, bring along a porta-potty, adapter seat, or his potty-chair.

Take Breaks

Make frequent stops along the way, and ask your child if he has to use the potty. Each time you visit a store or other place with a bathroom, ask your child if he has to go.

Make Toilet Visits

Check out toilets wherever you go. Compare them with other toilets you've seen, and discuss their similarities and differences. Many kids find toilets fascinating.

Bring Wipes

Bring toilet paper, tissues, or wipes so your child can clean himself when a bathroom isn't available.

Bring Extra Clothes

Pack extra pants, underpants, shoes, and socks in case of accidents or dribbles.

Public Restrooms

If your child is interested in public restrooms, let him check them out. Remind him to use caution to avoid germs, and make sure he washes his hands thoroughly after using the toilet.

Go Outside!

If there isn't a bathroom available and you don't have a potty-chair, show your child how to urinate outdoors in a safe, out-of-the-way place. This isn't something you want to encourage, but it is kind of fun!

Quick Tip

My friend was a recently divorced young father who had custody of his two-year-old son. At nineteen, he wasn't very tuned in to his son's bodily rhythms, but he did sense that the boy might be showing signs of being ready to use the toilet. So he bought a mock toilet seat that latched onto the rim of the toilet. The seat was shaped like a duck with a giant yellow head, a smiling bill, and protruding green eyes. The first few days of training went well. But one night he announced to his son, "It's time to go sit on the duck." The boy froze, his face went pale, and he screamed, "Nooooo!" For some reason, the duck that at first seemed friendly had suddenly become a grotesque monster. So they got rid of it. The boy soon adjusted to the big toilet and all was well.

—Tracy O.

Helping Your Child Stay Dry Overnight

Once you've conquered daytime dryness, you may want to see if your child is ready to stay dry overnight. This usually takes more time, but some children learn soon after daytime training is over. It can take days, weeks, months, or years.

Bed-wetting affects 10–20 percent of five-year-olds and 5–10 percent of ten-year-olds. It's usually hereditary and is more common in boys, although it affects girls, too. It can be caused by slow maturation, physical problems, fears, deep sleep, stress, allergies, illness, a small bladder, hormone deficiencies, and an insensitivity to the body's signals. Check with your doctor if you think your child has a physical or psychological problem staying dry. If you think your child is ready to begin staying dry overnight, here are some tips to help prepare him for success.

Prepare the Bed

Protect the mattress by lining it with a waterproof cover. You may also want to place a waterproof pad under the sheet in the area where your child usually sleeps, so you don't have to wash the mattress cover each time your child has an accident.

Buy Thicker Pants

If your child wants to wear training pants instead of pull-up diapers, you may want to buy ones that are thicker and more absorbent. If your child has a little dribble before getting to the toilet, he'll be less likely to wet the sheet.

Reduce Liquid Intake

Try to reduce your child's fluid intake in the hours before bedtime. If your child insists on having a drink near bedtime, give him smaller amounts to satisfy his thirst.

Make One Last Trip

Just before your child goes to sleep, remind him to go to the potty one last time to help him stay dry overnight.

Get Up in the Middle of the Night

You might want to gently rouse your child for a trip to the potty in the middle of the night, preferably when you're getting up to do the same. This works for some parents and children, but not for all.

First Thing in the Morning

Try to get your child in the habit of using the potty first thing in the morning. If your child isn't an early riser and is still wetting the bed, help him make a trip to the potty in the early morning hours, then let him go back to sleep for a while.

Offer Praise

When your child stays dry all night, give him lots of positive reinforcement. If he wets the bed, tell him it's okay. Tell him he can try again the next night.

I waited until my kids started to wake up dry in the morning before I switched them to overnight training pants. When they went a week without an overnight accident, I took them out of training pants forever.

—Kathleen F.

If Your Child Wets the Bed

The most important thing to do is not make a big deal out of it. Keep your child's self-esteem intact by never teasing, labeling, or punishing him. Don't talk about it constantly, don't compare him to other children, and don't get mad or act disappointed. Bed-wetting is quite common; it's just not talked about very much. Here are some reasons why your child might wet the bed if he's over the age of four or five.

Late Maturing

Some children are slower to develop than others. Your child's maturation clock may be set at a different time than other children. He'll catch up eventually; just be patient.

Insensitivity

Some children don't feel the urge to go as intensely as others, perhaps due to a slower-developing central nervous system. As your child matures, his sensitivity should increase.

Deep Sleep

Some children sleep so deeply they can't wake up to use the toilet. Sometimes they dream about using the toilet, which causes them to urinate in bed. This is something children outgrow in time, but they may need middle-of-the-night bathroom trips to help them get over the hurdle.

Genetic Predisposition

Some children wet the bed because of an inherited predisposition toward bed-wetting. If both parents wet the bed as kids, chances are good that their child will, too. When dealing with your child's situation, provide plenty of sympathy, and (if you were a bed-wetter) keep in mind how it felt.

Lots of Urine

Some children produce excessive urine during the night and may need medication to help control their output. Ask your doctor about DDAVP tablets, which contain a hormone that controls urine production. (See page 94.)

Super Stress

Some children experience a temporary bed-wetting problem when they go through a stressful event such as their parents' divorce, a new baby in the family, a new daycare provider, a new home, and so on. This type of bed-wetting usually disappears when the stress is eliminated.

Dry Sleepovers

Some children wet the bed when sleeping in unfamiliar environments, even if they've been staying dry up to that point. Talk to your child about any sleepovers coming up, and let him know that you've taken measures to prevent his embarrassment in case an accident occurs.

Alert the Parents

Call the parents ahead of time and tell them your child is still being toilet trained, so they can take necessary precautions such as protecting the mattress with a waterproof pad or mattress cover. (Ask them to be discreet about this.) Also ask the parents to prohibit any teasing if your child has an accident.

Use Thick Training Pants or a Pull-Up Diaper

Give your child as much protection as he wants. If he refuses to wear a pull-up diaper, give him thick underpants instead. Also include an extra set of clothes in case there's an accident.

Have a Chat

Talk to your child about the options. Ask him if he'd like to take his potty-chair, adapter seat, or another piece of equipment. Talk to him about using the strange toilet, that he can do it, and that he should ask for help if he needs it.

Quick Tip

My major toilet-training battle was getting my daughter to use the toilet when she didn't really have to, such as before a trip or before bedtime or nap time. These moments would always end in a fight. One day I told her that sometimes pee-pee is sneaky. It hides, and when you don't have a toilet around, it tries to sneak out. I told her if she doesn't get it out ahead of time, it may sneak out and cause an accident. So now whenever we're getting ready for bed or preparing to leave the house, we get on the potty and tell that pee-pee to GET OUT OF THERE! It works like a charm!
—Kelly S.

When to Talk to Your Doctor

If you're concerned that your child's bed-wetting may be a medical problem, and/or if your child is over six years old, your doctor may be able to prescribe a medication called Desmopressin Acetate (DDAVP), an antidiuretic that suppresses the kidneys from making urine for a period of time. The medication comes in tablet form and is easy to use. However, it's expensive, it may have side effects, and your child may experience a relapse after its use is discontinued.

Here are other reasons why you may want to talk to your doctor about your child's toileting behavior:

- Your child hasn't had a bowel movement in three days.
- Your child hasn't urinated in twelve hours, or is going infrequently (every four hours) with low urine output.
- Your child urinates very frequently (every half hour).
- Your child strains when urinating or defecating.
- Your child experiences pain when using the toilet.
- Your child uses the toilet but also wets his underwear frequently (every other time).
- Your child is over the age of four and still isn't toilet trained.
- You suspect something is wrong with your child's ability to toilet train.

Quick Tip

My daughter just turned three and is basically toilet trained except for pull-ups at night. I was discussing this situation with a parent friend of mine, and we decided that as long as daytime training is done, we're not going to get stressed out about the overnights. We're fairly sure our kids will eventually figure out that pull-ups aren't cool.

—Kelly S.

The Bottom Line

Remember to keep the following points in mind throughout the toilet-training process.

Don't Push.

Encourage your child; don't force him.

Don't Expect Too Much at Once.
Like any learning experience, toilet training takes time.

Don't Let It Become a Control Issue.
Work as a team, not as opponents.

Stay Positive.
This is an exciting time for both of you. Enjoy it!

Make It Fun.
Toilet training doesn't have to be work.

Remember That Your Child Will Be Toilet Trained Some Day!
Keep your eye on the big picture.

Quick Tip

We set the potty-chair in the bathroom for a couple of weeks so our daughter could get used to seeing it without any pressure. We talked about its purpose, compared it to the big toilet, and told her the potty-chair was her very own. We told her that when she was ready, she could learn how to use it. When she first tried, she clearly didn't like the idea, so we stopped for a week or two. When she tried again, she had immediate success. I think children need to get used to new things without feeling pressured to accept them. A positive attitude is the key to success. If it isn't a big deal for parents, it won't be for kids either.

—Gay C.

☺ Doll Play ✋

Some children are particularly sensitive during toilet training, especially about perceived failings on their part. This can happen despite parents' best efforts to keep things low-key. Doll play allows your child to express frustrations he may be having, and it gives you the opportunity to provide additional reassurance. By using a doll as a third party, you can provide your child with indirect (but much needed) help.

Sample Dialogue for Doll Play

While you're playing house with your child, you might say, "Oh, my! I think Dolly got so busy having friends over for a tea party, she forgot to go potty. It looks like she wet her pants! But that's okay. We can help her get into dry clothes. I bet next time she'll try harder to remember to go before it's too late!"

You could also say, "For some reason Dolly doesn't seem to want to go poopie in the potty, only pee pee! Did you notice she hid in the corner last time she had to go poopie? Let's ask her when she thinks she'll be ready to try going poopie on the potty. And let's tell her how excited we are for her, because it will feel so good to have clean panties after she goes poopie!"

If you're traveling, doll play can help your child learn to try new toilets. You can say, "Let's make sure Dolly takes a potty break. Do you think Dolly will enjoy trying a different potty?"

Doll play can also be used to promote overnight dryness. You can say, "Let's tuck Dolly in and remind her that she should think about waking up dry. Why don't we let her go to sleep without an overnight diaper! Dolly, you can put a sticker on your chart in the morning if you wake up dry! Won't that be fun?"

Ask Dr. Kelly

Question: My wife and I liked the idea of offering rewards for successful trips to the toilet, and our two-year-old adored the treats that were delivered whenever she put poops in the potty. However, now she tries to poop only tiny amounts so she can go more often and rack up more rewards. We're concerned that she may be harming herself by not evacuating fully. What should we do?

Answer: First of all, take pride in what a bright daughter you have! She figured out how to increase her rewards by increasing her number of poops. She should also figure out—on her own, and fairly soon—that she feels much better when evacuating fully. However, if she persists in passing only tiny amounts, adjust your reward system to reward only sizeable poops. If she tries to pass more but can only manage a little at a time, you'll want to talk to your doctor about the possibility of constipation.

Question: Our four-year-old daughter has been day trained since she was two-and-a-half, and now she's dry many nights as well. I'd like to get her out of pull-ups at night, but I'm reluctant to wash sheets all the time. Is there anything we can do to help her be consistently dry all night?

Answer: Once your daughter is dry most mornings, positive reinforcement may help. Consider letting her put a star or sticker on a calendar whenever she wakes up with a dry diaper. However, if she wakes up wet most mornings, such reinforcement will probably be futile. I would wait for her pull-up to be dry most mornings. Once this happens, you may want to talk with her before bed about waking up with a dry diaper. The power of positive thinking may be all she needs.

Question: My niece is so proud of having successfully trained herself to use the toilet. However, while we were out together recently on a shopping trip, she suddenly grabbed her groin area, did a dance up and down, and began crying that her "peepee" hurt. I rushed her to the ladies' room, where she was able to urinate only a tiny bit. She remained quite uncomfortable, but she didn't seem to have a fever. What was the matter?

Answer: These symptoms indicate a possible urinary tract infection. A fever may not always be present. Your niece needs to be examined, and a urine specimen needs to be obtained under sterile conditions. A urinalysis can be run right away to provide hints of an infection. If things are very suspicious looking, medication can be started before the test results come back. Soaking in the tub may help soothe the area. You can also have her use a squirt bottle to spray room-temperature water on her bottom while she's urinating, to help reduce the burning sensation.

Question: Our son conquered toilet training easily—both daytime and nighttime—the week after he turned two. However, at age three-and-a-half, he's suddenly begun soaking his bed at night. He eats and drinks up a storm during the day, and he makes hourly trips to the bathroom. I've tried to limit his fluid intake, but he's insatiable. What can I do?

Answer: First of all, you should allow your son to quench his thirst. He may be going through a stage, but I'm concerned that his symptoms display all the features of the onset of juvenile diabetes. If he's losing weight despite a huge increase in appetite, he should be seen right away and tested for high sugar in his urine and blood. Although this condition is uncommon, it's important to diagnose it early to avoid a more serious and threatening situation if detection is delayed.

Question: Our son is five years old now, and his pull-up is saturated every morning. We've tried restricting liquids after dinner and taking him to the bathroom when we go to bed at eleven o'clock, but nothing seems to work. Will he ever be night trained?

Answer: Yes, at some point your son will be night trained. About 20 percent of five-year-olds are wet at night. Each year thereafter, about 15 percent of bed-wetters outgrow the problem. Less than 1 percent of adults continue to have trouble. Most night-wetters are very deep sleepers, and many come from a family with a history of bed-wetting. Until your son is six or seven, I wouldn't intervene. However, if he's beginning to be invited on sleepovers or if he wants to go to summer camp, you may want to talk to your doctor. Several interventions are available, such as bed alarm systems and temporary, intermittent use of DDAVP tablets. Time and patience, however, are usually all that's needed.

Appendix I

Checklists

To help make toilet training even easier, here are some checklists you can photocopy or tear out and tape to the wall in the bathroom, kitchen, family room, or wherever you need a quick reference to the basic toilet-training steps.

Physical Signs of Readiness
❑ Has increasingly regular, predictable elimination habits
❑ Is staying dryer for longer periods of time
❑ Can sit comfortably on the potty-chair
❑ Can use a stepstool to climb on and off the big toilet
❑ Can pull her pants down and back up again

Cognitive Signs of Readiness
❑ Is aware that she's wet or soiled, or is about to fill her diaper
❑ Has a longer attention span (several minutes at a time)
❑ Can follow simple directions
❑ Can use language or gestures to communicate
❑ Understands the concept of using the toilet
❑ Knows toilet terminology and can identify relevant body parts
❑ Dislikes being wet or soiled

Psycho-Social-Emotional Signs of Readiness
❑ Knows she is a separate person
❑ Is curious about the toilet
❑ Has imitated someone using the toilet
❑ Is emotionally ready (no big stresses in her life)
❑ Appreciates praise
❑ Is eager to be a "big kid"
❑ Can engage in imaginary doll play

Potty-Chair/Adapter Seat
❏ Sturdy
❏ Safe
❏ Comfortable
❏ Portable
❏ Lightweight
❏ Easy to clean
❏ Easy for your child to use

Training Clothes
❏ Vinyl or plastic training pants
❏ Pull-up diapers (optional)
❏ Easy to pull on and off
❏ Big-kid underpants
❏ Ample supply
❏ Go naked (optional)

Accessories
❏ Baby doll (preferably one that drinks and wets)
❏ Decorations for potty-chair
❏ Toilet paper
❏ Toddler wipes
❏ Paper towels/cloth towels for cleanup
❏ Toilet targets
❏ Food coloring
❏ Amusements (music, books, toys)
❏ Rewards (stickers, stars, candy, small toys)

Setting the Stage
❏ Chat about the process.
❏ State your expectations.
❏ Discuss the benefits.
❏ Choose your vocabulary.
❏ Show your child the props.
❏ Pledge to work together with your child.

❑ Read books and watch videos.
❑ Be a role model.
❑ Watch your child's elimination patterns.
❑ Plan the beginning of the event.
❑ Choose a good time.
❑ Rehearse the process.
❑ Choose a doll.
❑ Offer positive reinforcement.

Time to Go
❑ Choose a free day.
❑ Dress your child in transition clothes.
❑ Motivate your child.
❑ Check often for signs.
❑ Use potty prompts or reminders.
❑ Make frequent visits.
❑ Expect accidents, and deal with them calmly.
❑ Go together.
❑ Use the doll.
❑ Praise your child's progress.

Step-by-Step Process
❑ Ask your child if she has to go.
❑ Move to the toilet room.
❑ Pull down pants and underpants.
❑ Sit carefully on the toilet.
❑ Offer entertainment (books, music, songs, conversation).
❑ After she goes, praise her.
❑ Measure the toilet paper.
❑ Wipe correctly (front to back).
❑ Get off the toilet.
❑ Pull up underpants and pants.
❑ Flush the toilet, or remove the potty-chair bowl and dump it in the toilet.
❑ Wash hands.
❑ Offer more praise and a reward.

Keep Going
❑ Continue with reminders.
❑ Continue with praise and rewards.
❑ Make it fun.
❑ Expect accidents.

Troubleshooting
❑ Check your child often.
❑ Change trainers periodically.
❑ Change sites.
❑ Increase rewards.
❑ Control fluid intake.
❑ Downplay accidents.
❑ Stay positive.
❑ Delay the process, if necessary, and try again later.
❑ Keep in mind your child will be potty trained some day!

Staying Dry Overnight
❑ Prepare the bed.
❑ Put on thicker pants.
❑ Control fluid intake.
❑ Make a last trip to the toilet.
❑ Use the potty during the night.
❑ Go first thing in the morning.
❑ Praise success.
❑ Avoid criticism.
❑ Talk to your doctor if you're concerned.
❑ Remember that overnight dryness takes longer.

Appendix II

Resources

Here are some supplemental materials that might help you during your toilet-training sessions.

Books for Parents

Mommy! I Have to Go Potty! Jan Faull (Raefield-Roberts, 1996)
Parenting Guide to Toilet Training, Anne Krueger (Ballantine, 2001)
Toilet Training, Vicki Lansky (Dimensions, 2002)
Toilet Training in Less Than a Day, Nathan Azrin (Pocket Books, 1989)
Toilet Training without Tears, Charles Schaefer (Dimensions, 1997)

Books for Parents and Kids

Dry All Night: The Picture Book Technique That Stops Bedwetting, Alison Mack (Little Brown and Co., 1990)
Toilet Learning: The Picture Book Technique for Children and Parents, Alison Mack (Little Brown and Co., 1983)

Books for Kids

Everyone Poops, Taro Gomi (Kane/Miller, 1993)
Going to the Potty, Fred Rogers (Dimensions, 1997)
I Have to Go! Robert Munsch (Dimensions, 1999)
I Have to Go, Sesame Street Toddler Books (Random House, 1990)
I Want My Potty, Tony Ross (Kane/Miller, 1988)
I'm a Potty Champion! Kitty Higgins (Dimensions, 1999)
Koko Bear's New Potty, Vicki Lansky (Book Peddlers, 1997)
No More Diapers, Emma Thompson (Dimensions, 1999)
Once Upon a Potty, Alona Frankel (HarperCollins, 1999)
Potty Time, Betty Reichmeier (Dimensions, 1988)
Princess and the Potty, Wendy Cheyette Lewison (Dimensions, 1998)
Toddler's Potty Book, Alida Allison (Dimensions, 1992)

Toilet Book: Don't Forget to Flush, Jan Pienkowski (Dimensions, 1994)
Uh Oh! Gotta Go! Bob McGrath (Dimensions, 1996)
What Do You Do with a Potty, Marianne Borgardt (Dimensions, 1994)
What to Expect When You Use the Potty, Heidi Murkoff
    (Dimensions, 2000)
Your New Potty, Joanna Cole (Dimensions, 1989)

Videos
Bear in the Big Blue House (Columbia Tristar, 1997)
I Can Go Potty (Consumervision, 1999)
It's Potty Time (Learning Through Entertainment, 1990)
Let's Go Potty! (Tapeworm, 1997)
Once Upon a Potty for Her/Him (Barron's Educational, 1990)
Toilet Training Your Child (Consumervision, 1996)

Internet Sites
www.babiesonline.com
www.childfun.com
www.dadmag.com
www.earlychildhood.com
www.family.go.com
www.iparenting.com
www.keepkidshealthy.com
www.parenting.com
www.parentingpress.com
www.parentsplace.com
www.positiveparenting.com
www.theparentingcenter.org

www.babytalk.org
www.childhoodresources.com
www.drspock.com
www.families-first.org
www.healthyplace.com
www.ivillage.com
www.parentcenter.com
www.parentingme.com
www.parentsoup.com
www.parentstages.com
www.pottytrainingsolutions.com
www.toddlerstoday.com

Dolls That "Wet"
Baby Born Doll ($48.00)
Aquini Drink and Wet Baby Doll ($19.95)
Pee-Wee Potty Doll, thepottystore.com ($12.95)

References

1. *Infant Care*, United States Children's Bureau, 1935.
2. T. McAuliffe, "First of a Kind Study Leads to Better Understanding of Toilet Training Process," presented at the Pediatric Academic Societies' Annual Meeting by Timothy R. Schum, M.D., Medical College of Wisconsin, 1999.
3. Ibid.
4. Ibid.
5. Ibid.
6. N. Blum, B. Taubman, and M. Osborne, *Pediatrics*, 99:54–8, 1997.
7. Ibid.
8. A. Thomas and S. Chess, *Temperament and Development: New York Longitudinal Study*, New York: Brunner/Mazel, 1984.

Index

A

Accidents
  child cleaning up after, 83
  deliberate, 84, 87
  expecting, 70
  not making a big deal of, 87
  parents' preconceptions of, 15
Activity level of child, 17
Adaptability of child, 18
Adapter seat for toilet, 37–8, 81, 102
Age of toilet training, 5–6, 25
  See also Readiness
At-home vacation, 57–8
Attention span of child, 18, 28

B

Baby, new, 12
Babysitters, 87
Bed, preparing, 90
Bed-wetting, 90, 92–3
Behavior issues, 83–4, 86
Body parts, naming, 59–60
Books on toilet training, 54, 76, 105–6
Bowel movements
  child's curiosity about, 16
  constipation and, 36
  "hiding" behavior for, 83
  holding back, 87
  patterns of, 27
  rewards for, 98
  vocabulary for, 8–9
  See also Elimination
Boys. *See* Gender differences
Brazelton, T. Berry, 5

C

Charts, 66–67
Child(ren)
  behavior issues in, 83–4, 86
  disabled, 19–20
  first-born versus second-born, 22
  as guide for toilet-training readiness, 26

observing, 56–7
  signs for needing to use the toilet
    in, 66
  signs of readiness in, 27–30
  temperament types of, 17–8
Child development, 16, 26–30
Clothes, toilet-training, 42–4, 48
Cognitive signs of readiness, 28–9, 101
Communication skills (child), 28
Constipation, 36

D

Daycare, 87
DDAVP (Desmopressin Acetate), 94
Defecation. *See* Bowel movements;
    Elimination
Diapers
  expense, 12
  pull-up, 42, 57, 94
  returning to, 8, 74
  vocabulary used when changing, 22
Directions, following simple, 28
Disabled child, 19–20
Distractibility of child, 18
Distractions, 47, 79
Doll Play, 60, 97
  assessing child's readiness with,
    32–3, 61
  for choosing toilet-training
    supplies, 50
  dolls for, 106
  for praise, 82
  process for, 48–9
  teaching toilet-training principles
    with, 72
  transition to big toilet with, 82

E

Early training, 1–3, 5
Elimination
  patterns, 27
  recording habits in, 57

Also from Meadowbrook Press

✦ *365 Baby Care Tips*

If babies came with an owner's manual, *365 Baby Care Tips* would be it. Packed full of the information new parents need to know—from teething, diapers, and breast- and bottle-feeding to discipline, safety, and staying connected as a couple—*365 Baby Care Tips* is the easy, essential guide to caring for a new baby.

✦ *Busy Books*

The Children's Busy Book, The Toddler's Busy Book, The Preschooler's Busy Book and *The Arts and Crafts Busy Book* each contain 365 activities (one for each day of the year) for your children using items found around the home. The books offer parents and child-care providers fun reading, math, and science activities that will stimulate a child's natural curiosity. They also provide great activities for indoor play during even the longest stretches of bad weather! All four show you how to save money by making your own paints, play dough, craft clays, glue, paste, and other arts-and-crafts supplies.

✦ *Discipline without Shouting or Spanking*

The most practical guide to discipline available, this newly revised book provides proven methods for handling the 30 most common forms of childhood misbehavior, from temper tantrums to sibling rivalry.

✦ *Practical Parenting Tips*

The number one selling collection of helpful hints for parents with babies and small children, containing 1,500 parent-tested tips for dealing with everything from diaper rash, nighttime crying, toilet training, and temper tantrums, to traveling with tots. Parents will save time, trouble, and money.

We offer many more titles written to delight, inform, and entertain.

To order books with a credit card or browse our full

selection of titles, visit our web site at:

www.meadowbrookpress.com

or call toll-free to place an order, request a free catalog, or ask a question:

1-800-338-2232

Meadowbrook Press • 5451 Smetana Drive • Minnetonka, MN • 55343